GUIDE
Coaching™

A Leader's Strategy for Building Alignment and Engagement

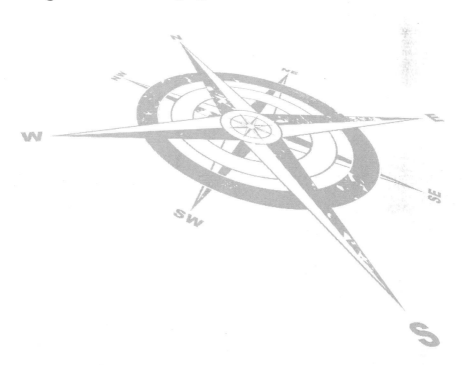

Ellen M. Dotts, Monique A. Honaman, Stacy L. Sollenberger

Published by ISHR Group
5400 Laurel Springs Parkway, Suite 303, Suwanee, GA 30024
www.ishrgroup.com

Printed in the United States of America.
ISBN: 978-0-9852955-0-9

What Business Executives Have to Say

ISHR Group has its roots in the corporate world and can clearly understand their clients' real-world needs. They are comfortable in global settings, even where language and cultural issues could exist, to deliver what the individual and the organization needs. Whether you are an emerging leader or a seasoned executive, ISHR Group can provide you with a pragmatic approach to leadership assessment, development and coaching.

Anne Abaya
Retired Vice President, Human Resources at
General Electric, and Executive Coach

We are in a current state where effective coaching is valued and essential to bring out the best in your employees. The well-thought-out content and examples in this GUIDE Coaching *book do in fact provide a great compass for impactful coaching.*

Bob Cancalosi
Chief Learning Officer, GE Healthcare

In an increasingly competitive and often volatile world marketplace, any business that hopes to thrive must achieve the optimal alignment and engagement of its employees. That takes great coaching; and not just by the top few, but by all leaders throughout your organization. That's where GUIDE Coaching *differentiates itself. Applying their unique and powerful coaching process, the highly experienced and talented authors of* GUIDE Coaching *offer organizations a widely tested and no-nonsense, practical model to effectively training and developing your leaders as coaches. Importantly, this to-the-point book shows you how to build a culture of internal coaching that can bring your organization that needed edge on your competitors.*

Bill Cooke
Director and Professor, School of Human Resources &
Labor Relations, Michigan State University

The ISHR Group has been a valuable partner to our organization for many years. Throughout our relationship, we've entrusted them to assess and coach some of our precious key talent, and their results have always been stellar. Their GUIDE method for coaching is a proven success. Now with GUIDE Coaching: A Leader's Strategy for Building Alignment and Engagement, *leaders everywhere can leverage GUIDE principles to improve the effectiveness of the human capital within their organizations. What a great resource for leaders!*

Tim Crow
Executive Vice President, Human Resources, The Home Depot

ISHR Group has assessed, developed and coached our leaders for many years as a true partner within our business. Their coaching expertise and "pay-it-forward" mentality truly highlights the depth of how to use GUIDE Coaching *as a competitive weapon for talent management and for creating a true culture of coaching.*

Sharon Daley
Vice President, Human Resources, GE Energy

Coaching, like all successful human resource development tools, requires a defined process to have sustainable impact within organizations. ISHR Group has taken their experience assessing, developing and coaching leaders around the world to create the GUIDE Coaching *model. The result is a practical framework and methodology to enhance leadership effectiveness and drive improved alignment and engagement within teams.*

Dennis M. Donovan
Vice Chairman, Cerberus Operations & Advisory Company, LLC.

I am a true believer that all leaders should participate in a "coaching" process. The practical GUIDE Coaching model allows everyone across your business to utilize a proven 5-step process that results in alignment and engagement that benefits both the coach and the leader, as well as your overall business.

Pamela Prince-Eason
President & CEO, Women's Business Enterprise
National Council (WBENC)

For years now, as a social researcher, consultant and speaker, I've been sharing eye-opening findings that impact how people want to adapt to certain realities in the workplace. But "want to" is the operative phrase. In applying any knowledge or skill-based content, we need great coaches — and the GUIDE Coaching model is an excellent tool to catapult good intentions into consistent habits.

Shaunti Feldhahn
Author, *The Male Factor: The Unwritten Rules, Misperceptions,
and Secret Beliefs of Men in the Workplace*

The need to build alignment and engagement within an organization is just as relevant with entrepreneurial ventures as it is with larger corporations. The most impressive aspect of the GUIDE Coaching model is that it works at any level and across any organization, function and industry.

Marsha Firestone, PhD
Founder & President, Women President's Organization

Through my own executive coaching, ISHR Group helped me to be more effective by asking the right questions and creating valuable insight into my strengths, my opportunities, and my overall leadership style. I was able to further translate this process into coaching my own direct reports to enhance their effectiveness and produce greater results for the company.

Rebecca Flick
Chief Financial Officer, SecurAmerica

I have worked with ISHR Group for 13 years and have utilized their leadership assessment, development and coaching services at every stop in my career — DuPont, Frito-Lay, ACE. No matter the company, the culture, or the situation, ISHR Group has always partnered with us to bring unique and effective solutions to help us achieve our goals. I am excited to see them continue to build on their successful GUIDE Coaching model and look forward to future projects together.

James Gibbs
Senior Vice President, Human Resources, US
Pharmaceutical, McKesson Corporation

I have worked with ISHR Group for more than 10 years and can't say enough about the quality of their work. In every engagement, they have approached the situation with a fresh perspective, not a one-size-fits-all approach, and have provided creative, practical solutions. Smart, extremely knowledgeable, innovative and tenacious — just a few of the adjectives I would use to describe the ISHR Group team.

Ashley Goldsmith
Executive Vice President, Human Resources, Polycom

GUIDE Coaching *is an outstanding approach for making effective coaching less of an event and more an embedded part of an organization's leadership culture. This book provides a practical guide for any leader who understands that the most powerful driver of business performance is a team of engaged employees.*

Brad Greene
Vice President, Human Resources &
Communications, Rexel Holdings USA

According to these very talented authors, "coaching is both an art and a science." In their GUIDE Coaching *book, they walk the reader through their contemporary yet time-tested model, which aims to achieve and sustain higher levels of organizational performance. It is worth reading and using as a reference tool, whether you are an experienced coach or a new leader. Well done!*

John J. Haggerty, PhD
Managing Director Executive Education, Cornell University ILR

ISHR Group is an outstanding business partner and an absolute pleasure to work with. Their high-energy delivery of proven leadership-development tools and executive coaching processes captured the attention of my group, who eagerly put the concepts to use and immediately discovered an enhanced team dynamic through improved communication. The results have been great!

Tonia Horton
Senior Director, HR Services, The Home Depot

Leadership is the key ingredient for success and growth in today's business environment. ISHR Group has the expertise required to help companies meet their needs for exceptional leaders. Their integrated approach assists organizations to identify, assess, and develop leaders to the peak of their performance in accelerated time frames. Investment in leadership development is a given in today's rapidly changing environment. By partnering with ISHR Group, companies ensure this investment delivers leaders that succeed.

Susan Hunsberger
Senior Vice President, Global Business Services, The Nielsen Company

So often the term "coaching" gets mistaken for "telling." Monique, Stacy, and Ellen have developed a framework for moving beyond the traditional and somewhat outdated process of "coach as director." They are to be commended for providing a simple, practical framework that gives leaders the tools and insights to be a true guide, advisor, and mentor in a way that develops the relationship between coach and leader. They have advanced the discipline of coaching beyond that of task accomplishment and into an arena of relational development that creates long-term, sustainable impact. The benefit is seen on all levels, from the individuals involved to the organization as a unit.

Joe Jotkowitz
Managing Partner, The Executive Advisory

We all strive to look for ways to continually drive improved performance, and GUIDE Coaching *reminds us of the power of building effective and engaging relationships. Ellen, Monique and Stacy offer a practical, straightforward, and focused model that will help anyone enhance their ability to coach others. Filled with uncomplicated checklists and real-life examples, this guide is a super book that you will be able to put to use immediately.*

Pamela O. Kimmet
Senior Vice President, Human Resources, Coca-Cola Enterprises, Inc.

As leaders, we all need that nudge to move us to the next level of engagement and alignment. Utilizing the GUIDE Coaching *model, ISHR Group shows you how to create a true culture of coaching within any work environment leading to a more focused and dedicated team.*

Roz Lewis
Executive Director, Greater Women's Business Council

I have had the privilege of working with ISHR Group for over five years. Their approach to leadership, their ability to engage an audience, and their regard for the value of creating an internal culture of coaching is amazing. They are a dynamic organization to partner with, and they deliver results.

Dave Pasternak
Vice President, Human Resources, Beacon Roofing Supply, Inc.

ISHR Group is my go-to organization for leadership assessment, development and coaching. As the leading authority on leadership development success criteria, they approach leadership with a passionate curiosity that enhances their expertise in providing their clients with pragmatic applications and solutions. GUIDE Coaching *is a must read for leaders of today and tomorrow.*

Rosemary Rivera
Executive Vice President, Human Resources, Americas, Sandvik

ISHR Group leads the way in assessing talent and coaching leaders around the world. Monique, Ellen, and Stacy have been contributing writers for Enterprising Women on the topic of building strong, effective leaders and engaging teams. Their message always hits the mark with the entrepreneurs and business leaders who read our magazine. I highly recommend GUIDE Coaching *to every leader.*

Monica S. Smiley
Publisher & CEO, *Enterprising Women Magazine*

I have worked with ISHR Group for years. They have provided coaching and educational services that are unmatched in the HR consulting arena. Intelligent, creative, proactive and contemporary is the best way to describe this team of professionals. Their assessment skills and delivery of solutions sets them apart.

John G. Waite
Manager, Human Resources, Mechanical Dynamics & Analysis, Ltd.

I have worked with the team at ISHR Group for many years, and they are one of the best when it comes to applying and teaching a highly effective and impactful, yet practical, approach to talent assessment and coaching.

Eileen G. Whelley
Executive Vice President, Human Resources,
Hartford Financial Services Group

"Our achievements are shaped by the terrain of our lives and the strength of the foundations we set. In building the life we've imagined, we must be true to our beliefs, dare to be ethical, and strive to be honorable. For integrity is the highest ground to which we can aspire."

Guide Coaching

Dedication

Thanks to our wonderful cadre of clients who we think of as colleagues and friends. Without your trust and willingness to welcome us into your organizations, none of what we do would even be possible!

Thanks to our incredible ISHR team comprised of the most dedicated, energetic, hard-working, and competent consultants and Coaches who represent our brand proudly each and every day: Stephan Altena, Shari Bracy, Amy Brink, Jennifer Buchholz, Shelley Hammell, Lisa Hart, Kelly Sack, Shelly Tomaszewski, Deanna Wilson, and Sherry Woodry. Without you, our story would not be the same!

Thanks to our husbands, Kevin, Justin, and Alan, and our children, Alex, Cori, Kendall, Harrison, Emma, Brennan, and Gavin, for all of your love and support as we have developed ISHR Group and this book. Without you, life would be boring!

And, we would be remiss not to thank each other for our genuine friendship and fabulous partnership. It's been said that friends can't work together, and we like to believe that we have proved that thinking wrong!

Finally, thanks to Successories, LLC. We believe in using quotes to reaffirm beliefs and to strengthen ideas. The quotes found at the beginning and end of each chapter come from, *The Best of Successories: Reinforcing Core Values,* and were personally selected to reinforce the GUIDE Coaching lesson. We feel privileged to share words that inspire us with those whom we hope to inspire.

With warmest regards and heartfelt thanks,
Ellen, Monique & Stacy

"Teamwork is the ability to work together towards a common vision, the ability to direct individual accomplishment toward organizational objectives. It is the fuel that allows common people to attain uncommon results."

Guide Coaching

Table of Contents

Guide Coaching

We owe a tremendous amount of thanks to the countless number of individuals with whom we have worked over the last thirteen years through our leadership assessment, development and coaching business. It goes without saying that we never identify and share personal information about whom we are coaching or about which companies we are serving. Much of what we deal with is confidential, as we work with individuals and with teams to leverage their strengths, and help them learn more about how to address their development needs. The key to an effective coaching relationship is a foundation of candor, confidentiality, trust and respect where participants are willing to talk, share, and let their guard down to be truly honest about how they can be most effective.

Our leadership and coaching services have taken us around the globe – literally. We have worked with Leaders across the United States and Canada, throughout Mexico and Brazil, across several countries in Europe, into Africa, through China and Japan, and into parts of Thailand and Australia.

Our clients range from multi-national conglomerates, employing hundreds of thousands of employees, to small, non-profit organizations boasting a staff of four. We have worked with entry-level Leaders, through C-suite corporate executives, and everything in between. We have worked across industries such as manufacturing, service, consumer packaged goods, technology, healthcare, banking, insurance and media. The Leaders we have coached have the same level of diverse backgrounds and experiences that we see within our client companies.

We thank each of you, individuals and organizations, for allowing us to do what we do!

"Achievement is not always defined by victory. Sometimes achievement lies in the honest endeavor to do your best under all circumstances, knowing that on any given day, intense personal effort may be the only thing that separates you from everyone else."

Guide Coaching

What is GUIDE Coaching™?

An alliance built on trust between a Coach and a Leader that focuses on strategies for the Leader to achieve optimal fulfillment, effectiveness and impact.

Definition – A strategic and collaborative relationship established for the purpose of moving the Leader toward achieving their situational, personal, career and/or life objectives.

Process – The Coach facilitates the Leader in defining their desired outcome, exploring options and ultimately making commitments to fulfill their desired outcomes.

Our Premise – The Coach's expertise is the GUIDE Coaching Process.

Ground
Understand
Incite
Decide
Encourage and **E**xecute

"The Coach is the guide on the side, not the sage on the stage."

Guide Coaching

Chapter 1
Why This Book?

"The power of perspective removes the rust from our minds and helps us to see beyond the box we've built for ourselves. Large obstacles seem smaller, long distances can be made shorter, and the unknown becomes familiar. Pausing to take a different view and appreciating everything more fully helps us understand where we are going."

Another book on coaching? Absolutely!

Why? Because we believe we are onto something really big and want to share it with you!

The focus on coaching for high-potentials is a relatively new phenomenon. It's safe to say that "coaching" has historically been viewed as something that was offered to you when your career was in trouble. People didn't want to work with a Coach, and if they were assigned a Coach, they more often than not kept that news to themselves. Today, working with a Coach has taken on new meaning. It's almost viewed as a status symbol. We hear our clients talk about working with their "executive Coach" just as much as they openly talk about working with their personal trainer at the gym. And the analogy is appropriate. Someone who works with a personal trainer does so to build strength which leads to sustainable health and longevity. Similarly, someone who works with an executive Coach does so to build leadership effectiveness which leads to sustainable engagement and fulfillment.

The Harvard Business Review article entitled, *What Can Coaches Do For You?* (authored by Diane Coutu and Carol Kauffman, published in

1

January 2009), speaks to this trend in coaching. The authors highlight that, *"Coaches are no longer most often hired to usher toxic leaders out the door,"* and instead cite the following as the top 3 reasons Coaches are engaged:

(1) develop high potentials or facilitate transition ... 48%

(2) act as a sounding board ... 26%

(3) address derailing behavior ... 12%

This is the bottom line and what we are excited to share with you: today's hottest trend is to develop coaching skills in and across the existing leadership team to ensure that all Leaders are able to provide coaching within their own organizations. This serves to create a true internal culture of coaching, which builds alignment and engagement within the organization. This "pay it forward" approach is ground-breaking, and we have had tremendous success introducing this idea to our clients.

First, let us provide some context. We are ISHR Group. Founded in 1999, we provide leadership assessment, development and coaching services to clients around the world. For years, we have provided coaching to our clients, and we have noticed the ways in which the professional landscape is changing. These changes are positive and will fundamentally refocus the way Leaders lead within an organization. The "I" in our "ISHR" name stands for *Incite*! To incite means to stir, to encourage or urge on, to stimulate or prompt to action! Our goal in writing this book is that we are able to "incite" you as a Leader to stimulate or prompt you to action — namely, to become a better Leader by incorporating the principles of GUIDE Coaching into your daily leadership routines!

Our writing mirrors our approach to business, our approach to coaching, and, frankly, our approach to life. We believe in letting our walls down and getting to know our clients to build deep, lasting relationships. We believe you have to focus on both leveraging your strengths, which differentiates you from other Leaders, as well as being aware of the areas you need to develop. We believe that everyone has a story that influences how they work, interact with others, respond to stress, react to change — and the list goes on.

At the core of ISHR Group stands a passion for developing Leaders. As our business has evolved, we have chosen to focus our service offerings into a trifecta that we define as assessment, development and coaching. We view these three areas as being fundamentally integrated and certainly not as stand-alone items (and you can learn more about our assessment, development and coaching businesses at the end of this book).

The "we" refers to the partners within ISHR Group: Ellen Dotts, Monique Honaman, and Stacy Sollenberger. Our professional backgrounds are grounded in the same approach. We all started our human resources careers at General Electric®, known worldwide as one of the most respected companies for developing Leaders. We did not work together while at GE, but our paths fortuitously crossed, and years later we found ourselves connecting around a common passion for leadership assessment, development and coaching. As with any coaching relationship, our styles are different, but uniquely complimentary. We value the differing perspectives that each of us brings to our business. Our similarities brought us together, but it's our complementary differences that make us so effective.

Why ISHR Group, and why GUIDE Coaching? Simply put, it's because we are experienced in working with Leaders. Our approach is practical, not steeped in theory. We believe in making a difference and in moving people forward with positive momentum.

Every one of our coaching engagements starts with what we call the *Grounding* "get-to-know" phase. This opportunity ensures that "chemistry" exists between the Coach and the Leader. We must make certain that the Leader is comfortable talking and sharing with the Coach and will respect the approach that is taken and any questions, advice, observations and feedback that are given.

We believe there should be a *Grounding* element to this book as well. With all of the business books on coaching that exist today, how will you know if this book is a good match for what you are seeking? It is about understanding who we are, and what we stand for, as that is indicative of the approach we take in coaching.

"GUIDE Coaching has been a great supplement and complement to my overall leadership development. Beyond learning hard skills, I improved my own self-awareness, which in turn has helped me to form and adjust my leadership style, ultimately making me a more effective Leader."

And here is our big difference: we do not think coaching should only be something that a third party completes with an internal organizational Leader. We do not believe someone should come in, coach, and leave without providing an opportunity to transfer those skills. We do believe in coaching and providing the tools to create a lasting culture of coaching within the organization.

Simply said, we believe in coaching Leaders, and we believe in teaching Leaders how to be Coaches. This two-part process is the key to our success, and frankly, the key differentiator of our business model. Sure, we can come in, coach a Leader, and achieve success in doing that as evidenced by a positive change in behavior. But, isn't it more valuable to come in and coach that Leader for the same positive change in behavior, while also leaving her with the skills to allow her to become an effective Coach within her own organization as well? This approach moves beyond coaching as a single element, and serves to create a true culture of coaching within our client organizations. Coaching one person is valuable. Coaching that one person to translate the coaching skills to engage and align others creates ongoing momentum with transformational impact.

We see coaching as a process for Leaders to become more effective in their own right, and also as a tool to engage and align their talent. This becomes absolutely crucial for Leaders who are leading or influencing other people (arguably something we all have to do).

This concept of employee engagement has created quite a buzz in recent years. Dr. Beverly Kaye, EdD., co-author of the best-selling book, *Love 'Em or Lose 'Em: Getting Good People to Stay*, has this to say about employee engagement: *"Many managers claim no responsibility for employee engagement and retention. They believe it's all about the money, perks and benefits, where they have little control. We know that's not true. In addition to fair pay, people want challenging, meaningful work; a chance to learn and grow; great co-workers; recognition and respect; and a good boss. The manager can influence these factors. Sometimes they know it … but need tools and processes to help them become more talent-focused."*

GUIDE Coaching provides those tools and the process that quite simply helps Leaders to become better Coaches. Together, this leads to increased engagement and alignment.

This differentiator mirrors who we are. It's a practical approach, and we're a practical organization. We get the world of leadership. We understand the world of business. We understand global implications. We understand the way things work within a corporation. We have played in this arena for years, first on the "inside" as we grew our careers within GE, and for the past 13 years as we have worked with clients around the world and across various companies, industries, and functions.

> "One, I was coached. Two, I was taught the tools to become a great Coach. This two-step process works. I felt what it was like to be coached effectively, and then I was able to transfer those skills to coach others in my organization."

One of our clients used these words to describe our strengths as Coaches and our belief in GUIDE Coaching: "executive prowess." We really liked this phrase and the image it conveys. It means we are respected by Leaders, senior Leaders and officers. It means we believe strongly in our approach and that we are able to convey that value to our clients. It means we have an inherent confidence in our GUIDE Coaching process. It works. We know it works. We have seen it work time and time again.

We did not make up the GUIDE Coaching process one afternoon over a cup of coffee. We didn't decide one day to call ourselves executive Coaches. Our "executive prowess" developed over decades of work in the industry and experience coaching business Leaders around the world. It comes from seeing that the process stopped when the coaching engagement was "done" and that the process could live on when we taught those same business Leaders how to be Coaches themselves. It highlights the adage of *"Give a man a fish, and he eats for a day. Teach a man to fish, and he eats for a lifetime."*

Our clients tell us we are different because we are more practical in our approach, we are pragmatic, we turn something that tends to be "mystical and intuitive" into something that can be taught, and adapted to others to fit their style. What do we mean by "mystical and intuitive?" When Leaders think of Coaches, they often think of "life Coaches," which for some creates images of "crystals and fluffiness." GUIDE Coaching is much more business-focused because it focuses solely on the individual. Our clients come to us to employ coaching as a strategic means to drive results for the individual and the organization. It is their reality. They need to drive sustainable, long-term business results. GUIDE Coaching is a strategic approach that has the potential to incorporate the intentions and goals of both the individual and the organization.

> "My Coach has vast experience dealing with people at all levels of an organization and at all points in their careers. She is able to bring this experience to the table and help me with my career. Examples of how this has helped are in framing realistic career goals, handling sensitive management issues, navigating a job search and articulating difficult communications."

We take the same powerful line of questioning that often accompanies life coaching, and we adapt it to fit within the framework of global organizations. Be it through delivery of a two-hour module or a two-day workshop on GUIDE Coaching, the feedback is consistent: we leave our audience with tangible skill development that they can immediately put to use within their business. It's immediate. It's relevant. People get resolution. They move forward. This is very identifiable. It's culturally transferrable. In our experience, all Leaders are trying to influence; all Leaders have a deliverable they are trying to accomplish; all Leaders have some level of strategic problem-solving, either for themselves or for others, which they are trying to accomplish.

Our aim is to translate those take-aways throughout this book as well. Our fundamental goal is to provoke the concept of coaching to hold the same resonance with corporate leadership as the concepts of effective customer service and bottom-line insight. We focus on deliverables and accountability. It's practical. People see results. Our goal is to drive results. We want to hear, *"That was a tangible result. I saw that benefit. That felt good. I felt the 'click' between 'heart' and 'head.' I saw what can happen when I change X."*

The majority of our coaching clients, probably 95% of them, are fast-track, highly promotable individuals whose companies want to provide them with focused attention to make them even more effective in the workplace by leveraging their natural strengths and learning to work around those areas that aren't as strong. Most of these people have been told at one point or another in their careers that they needed to delegate more and empower others, but often don't know how. Coaching is the how! When we can teach someone how to coach others on their team, suddenly the art of delegating and empowering others becomes much easier, and leads to greater success for both Coach and Leader.

Back to our initial question: why this book, and why now? Businesses are realizing that anyone can benefit from working with a Coach. It's often perceived as a form of reward and recognition. The reality is that you can't hire external executive Coaches for everyone. It's cost prohibitive. Our differentiator is that we fill the gap: we take what we know, we take what works, and we teach it to others. That is the gap that businesses have been looking to fill!

Who should read this book? Our message not only benefits business Leaders. Our strategies yield benefits for anyone who seeks to become more influential within their organization. It is not necessary to have direct reports to learn and apply the GUIDE Coaching model. We believe in the concept of the Coaching Pyramid, which essentially states that anyone can be coached – up, down, or sideways – to fit your needs.

> "In my role as a manager without direct reports, I assumed GUIDE Coaching would be a tool I would need and use some time in the future. I realized that it can be just as effective to coach up as it is to coach down."

This book is for anyone who works in an organization who needs to, or will benefit from, influencing others, working on his self-development, and the development of others (this is reciprocal!), needs to problem-solve, or help others to solve problems.

One doesn't need to be in a specific role or position within an organization to suddenly be deemed a Coach. Often, the best Coaches are buried within the organization while many at the top struggle to coach effectively and instead concentrate on directing their reports. Although straightforward communication is important, "telling someone what to do" is the antithesis of asking powerful questions, which is what effective Coaches do best.

Our coaching model simply requires five steps. As our methodology implies, "GUIDE" is the key word, thus:

Ground – This step embodies the essence of engagement. It is all about the Coach and the Leader establishing a relationship "beyond just business." This is where the Coach begins to understand what motivates the Leader in terms of her values, her vision for the future, and her goals. They also establish expectations and set boundaries around the coaching relationship.

Understand – In this step, the Coach and Leader gain mutual clarity on their intentions and vision, either for the short-term or long-term, or for their life or their career. They clarify those things that drive intentions and often serve to unknowingly confuse the issues and inhibit positive momentum. In some instances, the Leader may benefit from direct feedback during this time to gain a better understanding of the issue.

Incite – Here, Coaches are encouraged to foster multiple perspectives of the issue and various methods to address the topic being discussed. This is the "meat" of the coaching, and the point at which the Coach facilitates an exploration of opportunities and obstacles while analyzing various options. The pros and cons of each opportunity can be evaluated to drive commitment and to explore the best option for the Leader.

Decide – In this step, the Coach facilitates the Leader to make a conscious choice to achieve her vision by clearing the obstacles, confirming buy-in, and guiding the Leader toward the necessary next steps.

Encourage and Execute – As a final step, the Coach motivates the Leader to build upon the commitments made. The Coach builds confidence, provides encouragement, drives accountability, and generally acts as a champion to ensure the coaching session ends with positive momentum in place.

GUIDE Coaching is a process for coaching others, but it is also broad enough to apply to people who influence one another in a peer or matrixed environment. It's a process — and it's very flexible. In fact, we even hear from our clients that they use this with their friends and with their children (more often we hear it is used with teenagers because they appreciate that GUIDE Coaching is not condescending). Again, anyone can coach and anyone can be coached! GUIDE Coaching allows for proactive coaching (e.g., identifying feedback and how to deliver it in a coaching manner), in addition to general problem solving.

Does any of this sound familiar to you? Do you find it resonates with some of your experiences as a Leader? If yes, then this book is for you! We invite you to continue reading and learn more about what makes our GUIDE Coaching model unique and how to ensure you have created a culture of coaching that aligns and engages every employee in your organization.

"Determination is born out of purpose ... knowing that you are gifted for something and this something must be attained, it is never enough to rely on luck or natural talent. You must, above all, believe in yourself, face your goals, and then fight as if your life depended on it."

Chapter 2
What is in it for You to Coach?

"True leaders are not those who strive to be first but those who are first to strive and who give their all for the success of the team. True leaders are first to see the need, envision the plan, and empower the team for action. By the strength of the leader's commitment, the power of the team is unleashed."

You are a Leader.

You know how to coach your team, right? In fact, you coach them all the time. If that is the case, then your entire team should be fully engaged and aligned. Are they? If not, keep reading!

One of our fundamental premises within GUIDE Coaching is that coaching facilitates mutually fulfilling outcomes for both the individual and the organization. We believe that happy (yes, we said "happy") individuals are fulfilled in their lives, passionate about whatever it is they do with the majority of their time (for many, that's their job), and feel that what they do matters and is valued. Their "heart" is in the game, and they are passionate, rather than melancholy, about their work and their lives. Furthermore, their "head" is in the game, and their goals and objectives overlap or align with the organization's objectives. That is to say that what they do and how they do it is congruent with what the organization or their Leader expects. From an organization's perspective, these employees are "engaged and aligned" and are the "Rock Stars" of the organization because they deliver above and beyond, and always with passion. The reality is that many Leaders are really just managing from one perspective: the organization's. That's a critically important perspective for sure, but it is one-sided and, therefore, often not sustainable for long-term, mutually fulfilling success.

We begin by asking this question: *"Are you really coaching your team?"* By coaching, we mean strategically engaging them and ensuring that their goals and aspirations are aligned with the organization's goals. And, are they passionate about what they do and the level of personal fulfillment they feel in their roles? Are you sure they have both their "head" and their "heart" in the game? Are they motivated to deliver for mutually beneficial and fulfilling results? Do they believe that their contributions are making a difference?

Or, is the converse true? Do you think you are coaching your team when really you are simply giving your team advice or giving them feedback? Do you sometimes even feel like a therapist? Perhaps you find yourself on the other end of the spectrum and don't communicate with your team very often at all, instead assuming that you hired smart people who should know how to get their work done without abundant communication from you.

Coaching is an alliance that is built on trust between a Coach and a Leader and focuses on creating or formulating strategies for the Leader to attempt or practice in order to achieve a particular end goal which leads to optimal fulfillment, effectiveness and impact.

Coaching has many applications. On the one hand, it can be used to address performance. On the other hand, it can be used to compel someone to take action. Our GUIDE Coaching model recognizes the "whole person" and that each person has a set of experiences from which to draw upon that will impact the decisions that they make. We are all motivated by different values, experiences and desires, and what works in coaching for one person, may not work the same way to engage and align someone else.

Our philosophy is that anyone can be a Coach and anyone can be coached. There is no requirement for any expertise on the subject area. Rather, there is an expectation that the Coach will ask the right questions. As a result, this will drive the dialogue so that the person being coached – the "Leader" – is guided toward the decision that is best aligned with her goals and aspirations.

These decisions cover a wide range of coaching realms. These may include coaching to resolve a certain issue or to make a decision, coaching for performance, coaching for personal development, or coaching for fulfillment within career or life. Coaching is not to be confused with giving feedback and/or providing mentoring, which is a different subject requiring more formal relationships or expertise.

> "I used the GUIDE Coaching process to work through conflicting values and establish clear expectations with my direct supervisor. The process has also helped me to transform my direct communication into an indirect format that is less intimidating and more effective."

Why learn how to be a Coach? What is in it for you to consciously spend more time coaching your team, to take the time to really understand what is motivating each of your team members (vs. making assumptions based on your own perceptions and biases), and propel them towards becoming fulfilled and motivated top performers within the organization (or keeping them there)?

Leaders who truly coach and who create a culture of coaching within their organizations help build engagement and alignment. Many employees aren't engaged. They are bored. Their values don't align with those of the organization. They feel disconnected. They wonder about their purpose and the value they are providing. They may want to do their best, but they just aren't engaged or motivated. They don't have any initiative. They are merely the "Good Soldiers" following orders. Coaching an unengaged employee can lead her to understand more fully how her values align with the needs of the organization and instill a sense of purpose and passion.

On the opposite end of the spectrum are those employees who aren't aligned. They work hard. They have tons of energy, but that energy is misspent. These employees may spin their wheels by focusing on the wrong things and wonder why they don't feel in sync with their company. They become the "Rebels Without A Cause." They want to do what's right, but their energy is misdirected. Coaching a misaligned employee can help her to understand how best to focus her energies and her passions. This directed approach may lead her toward fulfilling commitments and adding value within her organization.

Here's a quick exercise. Look at the 4-block model below and mentally plot the people with whom you work:

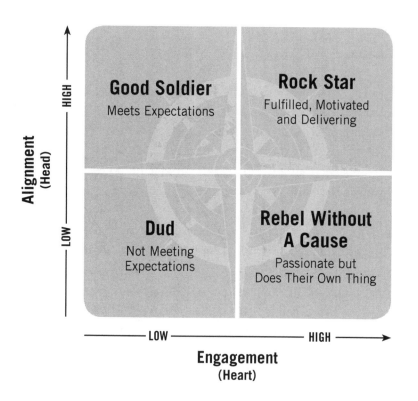

By "alignment" (the vertical axis), we are asking you to assess to what extent each person with whom you work is aligned with the goals and objectives of your organization/the company at large. In other words, is their "head in the game?" There may be many reasons why it may not be, but are you aware of what those might be?

By "engagement" (the horizontal axis), we're looking at whether their "heart is in the game." To what extent are they motivated, fulfilled and passionate about what they are doing every day?

Let's define each quadrant.

The Dud

This person has neither his "head" nor his "heart" in the game, but do you really know why? Perhaps you have already written them off or spent too much time trying to "fix" them? Coaching can help uncover the reasons behind poor performance to ensure you're addressing the appropriate underlying issue. This could range from an unsuitable position, to lack of training, to boredom, or a range of other issues outside the parameters of work. How often have you seen a superstar from one function promoted into a new role, only to see him fail? People don't typically tank overnight, but often times they are promoted into the "wrong" roles and nobody takes the time or makes the investment to discover the issue, but rather writes him off, fires him, or doesn't care when he ultimately quits. It might have been less costly (in time and money) to coach him through the issue and ultimately out of the poor performer box.

The Rebel Without A Cause

This person is a "diamond in the rough." He has great ideas, works hard, is passionate, means to do well, but isn't executing toward the goals you or the organizations have set. You need to harness his creativity, passion, innovation and ability to execute in order to create a top performer. Coaching can help you assess to what extent he understands and desires to be aligned with the goals and objectives of the organization.

The Good Soldier

This person does what you expect of him, but only what you expect and nothing more. These employees always meet your goals and objectives, but you know they can do more if they were just more passionate or demonstrated greater ownership. Why aren't they more motivated? Why aren't they as passionate about their job as you or others around them? Coaching can help uncover their motivational needs (which may be much different from yours) and resolve issues that produce a more engaged top performer. How often do you find someone just going through the motions at work, only to find him working like a "Rock Star" on a special project? What's the difference? Perhaps if you took the time to coach him you might discover boredom in the current role, and a true desire (and skill fit) to do something entirely different.

The Rock Star

This person has his "head" and "heart" in his game. His enthusiasm is infectious and causes others to want to "overachieve" as well. Having these folks on your team is wonderful, but they are also retention risks because they need to be continually challenged, and they need to feel fulfilled. Coaching can help you understand what else is required from a development perspective, either while in their current role or longer term. Furthermore, these are the folks that listen when the headhunter calls because they have heard about what a star they are. These are the folks that leave, without guilt, when they start to feel ignored, bored, stagnant, or unchallenged. In our experience, these folks benefit from "feeling the love" and the opportunities for continual challenge and growth. Coaching these folks is equally important and, in many cases, a key differentiator in organizations that outperform their competitors.

By plotting some individuals on your team against this grid, you can begin to formulate a reason why coaching might be beneficial (and also allows you to get to know them more as individuals!). We believe that there are opportunities to coach individuals in each of these quadrants. We have seen and been part of brilliant success with individuals in each of these areas, and it really is a remarkably rewarding experience for us and our clients. That is the beauty and practicality of GUIDE Coaching: it works!

As a Coach, you should also consider where you would place yourself on this grid. This is yet another perspective to recognize if you are considering GUIDE Coaching. How would you benefit from someone taking an interest in what fulfills you and where you would like to take your life and your career? Powerful stuff.

"Everyone has potential ... it is an infinite resource that cannot be exhausted, but can be lost in the clouds of fear and complacency. It may take courage to embrace the possibilities of your own potential, but once you've flown past the summit of your fears, nothing will seem impossible."

Guide Coaching

Chapter 3
Are You Coaching (vs. Advising or Mentoring)?

"People don't care how much we know until they know how much we care."

Does this scenario look familiar to you?

A team member, Laura, walks into your office and says, *"Do you have a moment? I really need some advice."*

You think to yourself, *"Well this is interesting."* Laura is a new Leader on your team and for the most part, she is self-sufficient and shows strong potential. You have been impressed with her ability to connect with her team, and she has built a positive reputation with your peers. Laura is a rising star, and you have high hopes for her to possibly take over many of your responsibilities as you expand yours. She has not come to you for much, so the fact that she is in your office strikes you as a bit unusual.

You could respond several ways, but let's look at one possible response:

You, of course, oblige Laura but must send that last email and your boss is waiting for that report, so you keep on typing. Laura knows how busy you are and will certainly understand that even though you are not looking directly at her, you are listening and most definitely care about her enough to give her some advice.

You say, *"Sure, what's up?"* Laura begins to tell you about an email she received regarding the "scathing style" of someone on her team and that many people do not want to work with him. This has produced a damaging effect on the team's ability to drive the project to completion. You have heard this all before, and you know exactly whom she is talking about. In fact, it's Liam again – he's known for his negative attitude, abrasive communication, and selfish approach that rubs everyone the wrong way.

You say, *"This is about Liam again, isn't it? Well, Laura, you need to do something about it. I have dealt with his type before and the way I have dealt with it is to show him what people are saying about him. You have got to show him that email and really address it this time. He is not changing despite other feedback. Just address it head on, Laura."*

Laura seems satisfied to have an answer as she quietly steps back and says, *"So you think I should just show this email to him? I'm not sure I can do that."*

Perplexed, you say, *"Seriously, Laura, that is exactly what I would do, and I have dealt with his kind before."*

You think to yourself, *"OK, another case solved. I sure am impressed with Laura. She will do great. Now, back to focusing on the other issue at the end of this email."* You are a multi-task master! You rock! No wonder you are moving up and on to better things.

Was that coaching? Are you confident Laura will follow through on the advice? And, what about next time? Will she be more or less likely to come to you for advice (and take more of your time)? There is no right or wrong answer!

You could handle this situation the way just described, or you could handle it this way …

You know you have to get that last email out. Your boss is waiting for that report. You also know that Laura is usually self-sufficient, so it must be important if she is coming to you for advice.

You stop typing, turn your chair to face her and say, *"Here, have a seat. Let's talk about this. Tell me more."* Laura sits down and you can tell by her body language (slumped, eyes down, and shaking her head) that this is really bothering her. She explains that she is concerned that others on the broader team, including your peers, are frustrated and do not want to work with Liam. You recognize that she is known as a strong Leader who supports her team and, you assume, she surely has handled "difficult employees" before.

"Laura, this is interesting because you are known for your supportive leadership style. Your team loves you, and you have a great reputation for your leadership. I'm curious, what about this particular situation bothers you so much?"

She responds, *"Yes — I do tend to give my team a lot of space ... my style is more 'hands-off' – and that has worked very well for me ... until now, because I haven't dealt with such a personality before. And, now that I'm really thinking about it, this situation bothers me a lot because I brought Liam onto the team. Everyone else I inherited, and they have been great. But Liam and I worked as peers before, and when the opening came up here, I hired him."*

You and Laura both begin to understand that Laura's dilemma is more about her reputation for having brought Liam onto the team and the strain it has put on Laura. This is directly related to her primary development need: conflict avoidance. You brainstorm with Laura to find different ways to address the issue. You consider firing him, doing nothing in hopes the issue will "go away," and having a candid one-to-one discussion with him. She evaluates the pros and cons of each option (e.g., firing seems too harsh while doing nothing yields the same result) and decides she needs to meet with him, give him the feedback, explain the impact of his behavior, and lay out what she expects to change going forward. She is energized, albeit pensive, about what she will do. She buys into the need to meet with Liam and clearly recognizes this as an opportunity to work on her tendency to avoid conflict.

Obviously, the second response is more "Coach-like." While it took more time, more curiosity, and more engagement on the part of the Leader, much more was accomplished, including greater buy-in and a commitment to action on the part of Laura. The Leader and Laura got "below the surface" and discovered the real issue: her reputation. In addition, the Leader was able to use the opportunity with Laura to address her key development area, conflict avoidance. Finally, Laura came up with the solution on her own with the assistance of some excellent coaching provided by her Leader.

We trust you are sufficiently intrigued about identifying opportunities to be more "Coach-like," but first let's clarify what we mean by "coaching." We recognize that Leaders wear many hats in an organization, and we are realistic enough to know that you are not just paid to coach. Leaders with whom we work have found our model helpful to define and differentiate the roles you have to play within your organization. There will still be many instances where you respond like the first example, but we also hope you will find more opportunities to step back and coach for a more sustainable and strategic result.

Many Leaders initially assess themselves as being good Coaches, when in actuality they are good tellers, teachers, advisors, or mentors. Let's ground our discussion by visually depicting the different hats Leaders wear in an organization:

Strategic

Mentoring
Strategic approach
to developing a less
experienced individual
by teaching, counseling,
sponsoring and/or
encouraging.

Coaching
Collaborative alliance
built on trust that
focuses on strategies for
the Leader to achieve
optimal fulfillment,
effectiveness and impact.

FOCUS

Directive ← RELATIONSHIP → Collaborative

Advising
Tactical intervention
using reinforcing feedback,
redirecting feedback and/or
advice for the purposes
of helping an individual
become more effective.

Therapy
Collaborative method
to understand the inner
dynamics of personality and
learn new ways of adjusting
and dealing with life situations.
**Should only be conducted
by licensed professionals.**

Tactical

Think of the vertical axis as FOCUS, beginning at the top with a strategic, big-picture or longer-term view, and ending at the bottom with tactical, day-to-day execution.

Think of the horizontal axis as RELATIONSHIP, running from the left with more directive or "telling" behavior, to the right with more collaborative or "questioning" behavior.

ADVISING: Let's start with the lower left quadrant, which we refer to as "Advising." The majority of Leaders spend significant time in this quadrant because of the nature

"I had been giving an employee repeated feedback about his overly-aggressive behavior. Normally, I would have just told him what to do, yet again — but this time, I followed the GUIDE Coaching process. It helped me to not only have him generate solutions, but enabled me to challenge him. Instead of simply saying, 'stop behaving badly,' I challenged him to 'surprise others' and be viewed as a role model in terms of collaboration. Within eight months he had completely turned around. It was amazing!"

of their roles. You are in a position of influence because of your past accomplishments. Your skills, abilities, and experiences draw others to ask for your help or advice, to give your opinion, or to offer feedback. Many Leaders feel they are good "Coaches" when they are actually good "tellers" (another excellent leadership trait, but not the reason you are reading this book!).

As is the case with Laura, the response and the interaction were quick and decisive. We are not saying that there isn't a time and a place for this scenario; we are simply saying that there are more opportunities for coaching, which yield more sustainable, long-term results, if applied in the appropriate moments. In the situation with Laura, the second approach yielded an action that was more meaningful and sustainable for Laura. Furthermore, the growth opportunity was identified and addressed for longer-term impact.

For example, this is what an Advising scenario might look like. The employee calls or emails manager with a problem ...

> Employee: *"I'm stuck on this issue ..."*
> Manager: *"I've had an issue very similar to this before, I think you should ..."*

MENTORING: As we move up the model, we come to "Mentoring," a term often used interchangeably with "Coaching," but one we believe is quite different because the premise is different. As a mentor, you are sought out for your wisdom (to be the "sage on stage") and experience. It differs from Advising because the relationship is based on the fact that the mentor has "been there and done that" and the mentee wants to emulate and learn from what you have achieved. The mentoring relationship is usually longer-term and often either career or "sounding-board" related (and therefore, not often successful in a formal reporting relationship). As a mentor, you are expected to "tell" or offer advice because that is more often than not what the mentee is seeking from the relationship. However, we believe that mentors can often be excellent Coaches by employing GUIDE Coaching to assist the mentee in crucial self-discovery. This way, their actions will have more personal significance and are less likely to translate as an order or request from the mentor.

This is what a Mentoring scenario might look like. The employee has a quarterly lunch scheduled with his mentor and asks for her opinion or advice …

Mentor: *"How have you been?"*
Mentee: *"Work is fine, but I'd love to get your perspective on a job I've been offered."*

COACHING: The upper-right quadrant displays the term "Coaching." It is still longer-term in nature, but the role of the Coach is not about "telling," but rather about "asking" the powerful questions to elicit the answers from the employee (to be the "GUIDE on the side"). This is not about advising what you would do in their situation, but rather about "teaching them how to fish" vs. "fishing for them."

This is what a Coaching scenario might look like. The employee calls her Coach and outlines a problem she is having …

Employee: *"I am tired of having to follow up with Taylor about deadlines and priorities. What do you think I should do?"*
Coach: *"What do you think you should do? What are your options?"*

Does it take more time? Yes! But consider the likelihood of the person returning to your office for the "answer" if they leave with the confidence that they can determine the answer for themselves. This translates into more time in your future, and a very practical way of empowering your team!

We are not suggesting that you stop advising and only begin coaching. There are situations that do not lend themselves as

"I am pretty independent, but I have found that my Coach provides things I can't provide for myself. She brings wisdom, experience, and a valuable perspective, and more importantly, knows how to guide me towards discovering what I really want and need."

coaching opportunities. Advising is more appropriate when there is a crisis situation, or when something is not open to interpretation. All we are suggesting is that before you automatically "tell" someone something, you bite your tongue and take three seconds. Ask yourself, "I could tell them what to do (whether it be how to address an issue or a development need), but is it a better use of my time to help them come to the conclusion themselves?" And, how much more motivated and invested towards the solution will they be when they have identified it for themselves?

THERAPY: Moving to the final quadrant, we find "Therapy." Try not to spend too much time here! We are not suggesting that you never let people vent about emotional issues at work or discuss personal issues: it is just a question of degree. At some point, we have all found ourselves in the position where an employee's issues should be referred to a licensed professional, or the conversation keeps being re-hashed without any resulting action.

In addition, remember that a main premise of GUIDE Coaching is moving the Leader forward, not dwelling in the past or focusing on the "woe is me." Your role as a Coach is to create momentum by identifying the opportunities (the vision for how they want things to be different) or viewing their situation from a different, more positive, perspective to get them "unstuck." The key difference between "Coaching" and "Therapy" is that therapy is focused on looking back at the past to uncover clues as to why the situation is the way it is. "Coaching" is focused on taking the person from their current position and propelling them forward toward their goals and objectives.

This is what a Therapy scenario might look like. The employee generally starts a conversation with something like …

- *"I'm having trouble focusing."*
- *"I'm not sleeping well."*
- *"I've been seeing a therapist and I need to talk with you about some things that are troubling me."*

The manager may think any of these things …
- *"I'm not equipped professionally to handle this situation."*
- *"This is the 4th time he has been in my office this week discussing the same thing without resolution."*
- *"I wonder if there is something in his childhood that is causing him to be this way."*

Our caveat here is that not every moment is a coaching moment. When Rome is burning (or someone is about to fall off a cliff!), you move into "telling" (and often "doing"!) mode. All we ask is that after reading this book you pause before you are about to "tell" and ask yourself, *"Is now the time to ask questions? Is this a coaching moment?"*

There are also topics that lend themselves more to coaching than others. A question that requires a yes/no answer or has a finite answer could be coached, but you need to ask yourself whether it is a good use of your time (e.g., *"May I take a personal day tomorrow?"* or *"How has this policy been interpreted in the past?"*). There may also be topics where you may feel uncomfortable as a Coach. It is likely that the Leader also needs advice from an expert and doesn't have all the answers within them. Trust your gut in these areas, and refer the Leader to someone with more expertise in the area (e.g., a therapist or counselor).

As a quick reminder…

Advising is … traditional "management," tactical, command and control, giving advice and telling (teaching or training may fall into this category, as well), and is usually done when there is a right or a wrong answer, versus an approach that may or may not suit one person or another.

Mentoring is ... strategic and based on the premise that the mentor has more experience or skill than the mentee, or that the mentee wants to emulate or follow in the path of the mentor.

Coaching is ... even more strategic and more collaborative. It doesn't require experience in the coaching topic, but does require a genuine interest in moving the Leader forward.

Therapy is ... collaborative and interested in fixing the problem. It's delving into the psyche of the individual to answer the "why" questions.

Now that we have laid the groundwork for the "leadership field" in which you are playing, let's look at our GUIDE Coaching model and process.

"Be the light that others can come to with their ideas, visions and dreams. Never doubt that blending your talents with those of others can change the world."

Chapter 4
The GUIDE Coaching Process

"Learn to embrace change, and you will begin to recognize that life is in constant motion, and every change happens for a reason. When you see boundaries as opportunities, the world becomes a limitless place, and your life becomes a journey of change that always finds its way."

When our clients began asking us how we coach and whether we could teach it to them and to others, we knew it would have to be simple, teachable, practical, and memorable. It could not be convoluted, complicated, "fluffy," or mired in too much detail. Furthermore, it needed to be effective and yield value. The reality is that most of our clients' time is in high demand and they would only settle for a practical process that yielded effective results quickly and efficiently. Clients who have learned and applied GUIDE Coaching tell us it meets all these criteria.

GUIDE Coaching is a five-step process by which you, as the Coach, guide the Leader toward an action or a decision. As you learn the process, it is important to keep in mind that it is best to keep it simple and follow the process — *because it works.*

Furthermore, it is imperative to distinguish that the Coach's expertise, unlike mentoring and advising, is the GUIDE Coaching process. The skill of the Coach is in asking the right questions to guide the Leader toward making a decision or taking an action that moves them closer to their vision. This is usually a huge eye-opener to Leaders as they learn the process. This bears repeating! The expertise of the Coach does not lie in their own personal experience. The expertise of the Coach lies in following the GUIDE Coaching process and asking the right questions to guide the Leader to take an action.

Let's face it, it is often difficult for Leaders to shift their paradigm from, *"I should have all the answers; that is why I am the Leader,"* to behaving as a facilitator of a process for others to "find the answer." In our experience, this is an extremely difficult "habit" to break. Most Leaders have experienced much success because they have had the answers! Furthermore, as Leaders know, the majority of their day is spent solving problems or giving answers to the plethora of questions from those around them.

If you think back on the people – the "Coaches" – who have taught you the most and had the most influence on your life and in your career, we would venture to bet that they were the ones who asked the most thoughtful questions – the questions that made you really think. They were the ones who made you feel as if they truly cared about you as an individual and valued your best interests. They were the ones that engaged your thinking so that you could assess and evaluate your own circumstances, dilemmas, and situations to come up with your own decisions or solutions.

The key is that the decisions or solutions came from you. While these most influential Coaches may have offered possible answers or ideas (and, indeed, gave excellent advice), it was you, ultimately, who came up with the solutions on your own. Furthermore, you were likely "bought-in" to the decision and apt to follow through and learn from the situation. In short, our process relies more on asking versus telling. It is imperative that you get comfortable with that concept as you learn the process.

Think of the best Coaches you have had in your life! They can be from school, from the workplace, or from outside activities, such as athletics or the arts. What did they say or do that made them good Coaches? Focus on observable behaviors. Be specific about the interactions you had with them.

Can you come up with five items that set them apart?

1. _____

2. _____

3. _____

4. _____

5. _____

What does your list look like? Are there any common themes that emerge? The fact of the matter is that most people who are considered great Coaches have commonalities in terms of how much they "cared about" and how much "time they spent" with the person they were coaching. Do any of these items resonate with what you put on your list?

- *"They were specific in their feedback, whether it was reinforcing or redirecting."*

- *"They cared about my success."*

- *"They took the time to get to know me."*

- *"They were available and accessible."*

- *"They allowed me to try things my way, make mistakes, and learn from them."*

- *"They asked more and told less."*

- *"They challenged — and sometimes even frustrated — me to do things out of my comfort zone."*

- *"They empowered me and increased my confidence."*

The GUIDE Coaching process builds on each of these. We will describe the process, and then we will explain the model behind the process to detail why it has proven to be extremely effective.

> **The journey is theoretically linear yet ambiguous in practice.**

G GROUND
Align and Discover

U UNDERSTAND
Articulate the Vision

I INCITE
Perspectives
and Possibilities

D DECIDE
Facilitate Their
Choice and Plan

**E ENCOURAGE
AND EXECUTE**
Support and Hold
Accountable

It is important to note that GUIDE Coaching is a five-step process, and while it is linear in theory, one must bear in mind that in practice, it is ambiguous. That is to say, the step may or may not be completed in one sitting, and you may go up and down through the step as necessary. This is an art more than a prescriptive science, but as best we can, we have created a process to follow. We will review this in more detail in Chapter 5, "The Art and Skill of Coaching."

Ground – The objective in this step is to get to know the Leader, establish expectations, build trust, and set boundaries. This is where the Coach begins to understand the context and what motivates the Leader in terms of their values, vision for the future, and goals. It is the "get to know" step that may have occurred over time or, if it is a new relationship (e.g., a new team member or peer), is a deliberate starting point in getting to know them.

In our experience, exceptional Leaders do this already. For some it comes naturally, while others have learned that knowing what motivates their teams and others with whom they work is a powerful means to fostering engagement, loyalty, and ability to influence. If it is a new team member or new relationship in general, this is an imperative step that takes some investment in time at the beginning, but pays dividends in the future.

This step can occur once or over time in a relationship. If you are formally coaching someone, or if the person is someone you coach frequently, you would obviously not need to complete this step every time. The question to ask here is how well do you really know the person you are coaching? Do you know what motivates them, their priorities, who they aspire to be, what they want to be known for, etc.? You may want to re-evaluate motivation over time because people change.

We recognize that studies indicate that there is a gender difference when it comes to this step. As a whole, women tend to *Ground* more easily than men. The lines between their professional and their personal worlds tend to be more blurred. The research shows that men, more frequently, separate the idea of blending their work and their personal lives. Our experience shows us that regardless of gender, our clients are more effective when they *Ground*.

"I never had a manager who was a good Coach, so I didn't understand the value of coaching. Now that I have personally benefited from coaching, I see the value of asking my team what motivates and doesn't motivate them, what they want from their job and career, and what they want from me. These questions, which may appear mundane or irrelevant, are so powerful. I now see things from their perspective and am more able to stand in their shoes."

Maya Angelou said, *"I've learned that people will forget what you said, people will forget what you did, but people will never forget how you made them feel."* In our executive assessment and coaching practice, we find this to be entirely true: the people you work with remember when you acknowledge them and make the effort to get to know them. Yes, while these are business relationships, the reality is that we are not robots – lacking empathy, feelings, ambitions, and a personal life – coming to work each day. In fact, we bring our whole selves to work with us every day. Inevitably, we all want to work in an environment where we are valued and feel that our contributions are acknowledged.

We have far too many examples of Leaders, both men and women, we have coached who struggle with building a following and have a limited ability to influence to ultimately produce sustainable results in their roles. The reality is that relationships matter at work, and those Leaders that build genuine relationships with their co-workers are more effective. Our friend, Joe Jotkowitz, Founder and Managing Director of The Executive Advisory, is a communication expert with whom we have collaborated on a number of leadership development projects. Joe introduced us to a simple, yet profound, exercise that helps Leaders identify where they have achieved or have failed to build genuine professional relationships. This "likeability index" can not only serve to help you connect with and coach those with whom you work, but it will also impact the credibility of your communications.

Using the diagram on the next page, fill in the names of key Leaders (e.g., your boss, your skip-level Manager, his or her peers at that level, etc.), significant peers, and team members. Can you answer these questions about each of them?

1. *"What is the name of their spouse or significant other?"*

2. *"Do they have children? If so, what are their names?"*

3. *"What are the hobbies and interests that keep them busy outside of work?"*

4. *"Can they answer those same things about you?"*

Managers

1. _____
2. _____
3. _____
4. Yes or No

1. _____
2. _____
3. _____
4. Yes or No

1. _____
2. _____
3. _____
4. Yes or No

1. _____
2. _____
3. _____
4. Yes or No

Peers

1. _____
2. _____
3. _____
4. Yes or No

1. _____
2. _____
3. _____
4. Yes or No

1. _____
2. _____
3. _____
4. Yes or No

1. _____
2. _____
3. _____
4. Yes or No

Team Members

1. _____
2. _____
3. _____
4. Yes or No

1. _____
2. _____
3. _____
4. Yes or No

1. _____
2. _____
3. _____
4. Yes or No

1. _____
2. _____
3. _____
4. Yes or No

As you review your diagram, notice if there are a significant number of blanks, or is your diagram relatively full? This is a good indicator as to whether or not you have truly engaged your co-workers and colleagues to build genuine, authentic relationships or whether you have kept it "strictly business." Many of the Leaders we coach are perceived as viewing their teams or their peers as "resources" as opposed to "individuals." They are perceived as building relationships simply as "a means to an end" as opposed to "an end unto itself," where relationships are genuine and intentional.

Time and again, Leaders ask us why it should even matter if they "connect" personally with people at work. We have had Leaders tell us that it is irrelevant if anyone knows who they are outside of work or what they stand for. Without any disrespect, they simply do not understand why talking about what they did over the weekend is of any relevance in the workplace. The fact of the matter is that opening up a bit personally, sharing who you are, and getting to know those with whom you work, allows relationships to develop … which leads to trust … which leads to loyalty … which leads to increased productivity and efficiency. It is a cycle that cannot be disputed.

We understand that for some of you, this may be a difficult paradigm to shift. However, we find time and again that the Leaders that make the effort to genuinely get to know those they work with beyond the "strictly business" boundaries are perceived as being more thoughtful, more well-liked, and overall more engaged as Leaders. When the opposite is true, and Leaders operated under a "strictly business" policy, we have found they have fewer followers, and they find it particularly difficult to influence within their business.

In any organization, let alone a highly matrixed organization, this causes long-term issues, and a "strictly business" style simply is not sustainable. A "strictly business" style is sterile, cold, and can come across as selfish when you need something from your co-workers. Bottom line? Try getting beyond "strictly business" and move towards building genuine relationships to see if it makes a difference. Remember, keep it GENUINE! Others will see through you if it is not sincere (e.g., that you honestly want to get to know them, not just to "fill in your likeability index"). While this concept may sound basic to some, or sound irrelevant to others, these questions provide practical support on how to develop relationships so often missed by many Leaders, yet so necessary to make coaching sunstainable and meaningful.

The objective of the *Ground* step in the GUIDE Coaching process is to get to know the Leader, build trust, set expectations, and the context around her circumstances.

We have found the following *"Grounding Milestone Checklist"* valuable for Coaches to review as they go through the *Ground* step with their Leaders. The first four sections are typically shared and discussed between both Coach and Leader, while the last three sections are typically focused solely on the Leader. You may find that this list is a great "assimilation" as you get to know new members on your team and as you embark on more formal coaching relationships.

Grounding Milestone Checklist

1. Backgrounds

- *"What got you here?"*

- *"Who is someone you have looked up to and why?"*

- *"What has been the most difficult situation you have faced? How did you handle it?"*

- *"What have been key influences in your life and how have they impacted you?"*

2. Aspirations

- *"What are your career goals?"*

- *"What are your life goals?"*

3. Values/Priorities

- *"What's important?"*

- *"How are you honoring values now?"*

- *"What do you want to work on/improve?"*

- *"Where do you want to find more balance?"*

4. Styles/Approaches

- *"How are we similar or different?"*

- *"How will this affect our coaching relationship?"*

5. Self-Assessment

- Strengths: *"In what areas do you excel, do well, or have skills that come naturally?"*

- Developmental Areas: *"In what areas do you have gaps, struggles, or lack skills that don't come naturally?"*

6. Developmental Goals

- *"What do you as a Leader want to work on?"*

- *"Can you explain the insight into why?"*

7. Coaching Rhythm/Logistics

- *"How often do we plan to meet?"*

- *"Where will we meet?"*

- *"Who will set up the next step each time?"*

- *"How will subsequent meetings be set up (e.g., via assistant, calendar, phone call, etc.)?"*

- *"Who has topic accountability?"*

- *"Who will be the note-taker?"*

Remember, the first step in GUIDE Coaching is all about *Grounding*: building trust and getting to know the leader.

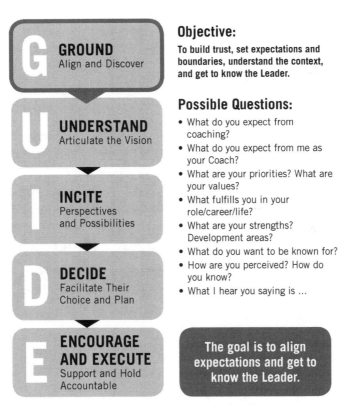

GROUND
Align and Discover

UNDERSTAND
Articulate the Vision

INCITE
Perspectives
and Possibilities

DECIDE
Facilitate Their
Choice and Plan

**ENCOURAGE
AND EXECUTE**
Support and Hold
Accountable

Objective:
To build trust, set expectations and boundaries, understand the context, and get to know the Leader.

Possible Questions:
- What do you expect from coaching?
- What do you expect from me as your Coach?
- What are your priorities? What are your values?
- What fulfills you in your role/career/life?
- What are your strengths? Development areas?
- What do you want to be known for?
- How are you perceived? How do you know?
- What I hear you saying is …

The goal is to align expectations and get to know the Leader.

Understand – In this step, the objective is for the Coach and Leader to gain mutual clarity on the Leader's intentions and vision for their desired long-term and/or short-term outcomes. For example, if the coaching is for career development (long-term), to where does the

Leader aspire? Or, if the coaching is regarding skill development, what is the Leader's definition of skill mastery?

This is a critical step in GUIDE Coaching because it is fundamental that the coaching is about the Leader, not the Coach. It is what distinguishes coaching from advising and mentoring. In other words, when someone comes to you because they are stuck, seeking an answer, or grappling with a decision, it is your role as the Coach to understand what the Leader wants, not to impose what you would do in the same situation or what you have done in similar situations. Remember, it is about facilitating the Leader to an action or a decision that works best for them, not you. It is imperative that both the Coach and the Leader are mutually clear on what it is the Leader wants.

"Someone came to talk to me about the fact that she was going to have difficulty managing a current peer if and when she took a promotion. Applying the process around GUIDE Coaching helped me to realize that her concern was only 'the tip of the iceberg.' The real issue was that she didn't want to take the promotion because it required relocation, but she didn't know how to have that conversation with her one-over-one manager. The end result was she had the courage to say 'no' and was true to herself, while still maintaining her professional reputation. She ended up receiving another promotion a year later that didn't involve moving."

Effective coaching requires more curiosity and questions than advising and mentoring roles. Curiosity and questions help you and your Leaders uncover that which is "below the surface." We often refer to the iceberg example in explaining this concept. In other words, when individuals come to us for coaching, what they often initially present as the issue, dilemma, or decision isn't the actual subject with which they are grappling at all. Instead, it is just the "tip of the iceberg" or the surface level issue. Think of it as perhaps the "symptom" to the real cause of their dilemma or angst. By being more curious and asking more questions, such as *"What about this really bothers you?"* or *"You have dealt with this before, why is this different for you?"* we can often uncover the greater issue with which they are struggling.

Furthermore, you can also begin leveraging what you know about them from *Grounding* to get below the surface. You might inquire, *"I know you too well. This seems like a simple issue for you. What is this really about?"* By using this approach, you acknowledge their predicament while recognizing what you are sensing: that there is more to the issue below the surface.

Recall the dialogue with Laura at the beginning of the last chapter. By observing Laura and getting to know her, there is already context when she comes in looking for "advice." However, by virtue of being curious, asking more questions, and leveraging *Grounding* to discover "what's below the surface," we were able to discern the motivating and underlying issue. It was her reputation for recommending and hiring the difficult team member.

Let's review another scenario that demonstrates the GUIDE Coaching steps in action.

Leader: *"Do you have a minute? I need your advice."*

Coach: *"Absolutely. What's up?"*

Leader: *"I just received some feedback that I am unintentionally creating an autocratic environment on my team. I guess I interrupt people, I don't solicit input, and I am too direct in my approach."*

Coach: *"First, I have to say that I can see this really bothers you. Tell me more."*

Leader: *"Yes, it really does bother me. I'm new in this role and I don't want to be perceived this way. I mean, I know it's my style ... it's how I got here ...."*

Coach: *"How do you want to be perceived?"*

Leader: *"I want to be perceived as facilitating decisions ... not forcing my ideas on the team. I knew this role would stretch me in this area, but it doesn't come easily to me."*

Coach: *"So you want to learn to flex your style?"*

Leader: *"Yes, definitely ... and learn how to draw out ideas and not shut people down."*

Coach: *"Why is this important to you though?"*

Leader: *"It's important because I have a reputation for alienating people, and I've got to change that if I'm going to be successful at leading a team. I can't continue to do it all myself like I'm used to doing. If I create an environment where everyone feels I have to have the final say, I'll never get anything done."*

Coach: *"What do you want to change then?"*

Leader: *"I want to change this perception and build a reputation for empowering my team and creating an open environment."*

By simply asking more questions and being curious, the Coach got "below the surface" and to the issue that was most meaningful and compelling for the Leader, the perception that she is not empowering her team and making an effort to flex her style. Furthermore, the Coach and the Leader gained mutual understanding of the Leader's desired outcome: namely, to build a reputation for empowering her team and creating an open environment. They both leave the coaching session sharing a mutual understanding of the issue and what the Leader wants, rather than coaching to a surface issue without a keen understanding of the desired outcome.

This step is also critical in fostering buy-in and commitment to whatever the Leader chooses to do. Effective Coaches hone in on "the hook." Namely, those things that are important to the Leader – their values and long-term objectives – which are often "below the surface." We learn what these key drivers are for each Leader from the *Grounding* step!

Proactive coaching is another method that can be effective during the *Understand* step. In this case, the Leader is not reaching out to discuss something, but rather you, as the Coach, are initiating the conversation. Typically, this occurs when you are giving feedback. This could be positive feedback to reinforce a behavior that you want to see more of, or re-directing feedback to course-correct an ineffective behavior. When you are giving feedback, you are not in "coaching" mode because your goal is to ensure clarity and understanding around the specific behaviors that you are observing.

However, instead of continuing to be in "advising" mode by continuing to "tell" your Leader what they need to do differently, try moving to "coaching" mode by asking the Leader what they think of the feedback. Let's look at an example:

Coach: *"Since you have been in your new leadership role for a month, I thought it would be a good time to touch base on how things are going, and I would like to give you some initial feedback. I've observed you in some meetings, and it appears that you are unintentionally creating an autocratic environment ... you interrupt people at times, you tend not to solicit input, and are very directive in your approach. I have also heard this from some of your team members who haven't felt particularly empowered or valued the past month."*

Leader: *"Who have you spoken to? I'm shocked since I have always prided myself on being an inclusive Leader. It's always been highlighted as a strength in my past roles."*

Coach: *"Who gave the feedback isn't important ... and remember, I have observed some of this behavior myself. As I mentioned, I'm sure it is unintentional ... perhaps an overuse of your 'passion.' What do you make of this feedback? What do you want to do about it? What's in it for you to try and change these perceptions?"*

Leader: *"Well, I know I interrupt people at times and I can try and 'bite my tongue' and force myself to listen more ..."*

Coach: *"What else can you try?"*

Can you see value of transitioning a feedback discussion to a coaching one? By beginning to ask open-ended questions, you are putting the responsibility on your Leader (taking the "monkey off your back!") for taking ownership of the feedback and associated behavior change. It is also a great way for you to assess where your Leader is in terms of self-awareness, ownership, and motivation to act (which are topics we will cover in more detail when we discuss "Context" in the next Chapter).

Remember, the second step in GUIDE Coaching is all about *Understanding*: being able to articulate the Leader's vision (not your own vision as the Coach), and gaining clarity on the desired outcomes.

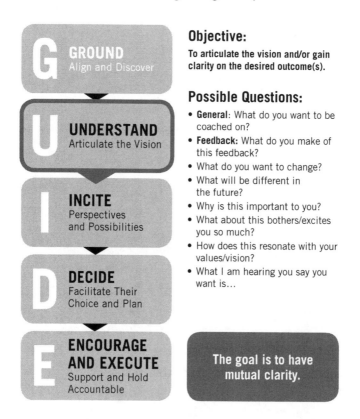

GROUND
Align and Discover

UNDERSTAND
Articulate the Vision

INCITE
Perspectives
and Possibilities

DECIDE
Facilitate Their
Choice and Plan

**ENCOURAGE
AND EXECUTE**
Support and Hold
Accountable

Objective:
To articulate the vision and/or gain clarity on the desired outcome(s).

Possible Questions:
- **General**: What do you want to be coached on?
- **Feedback:** What do you make of this feedback?
- What do you want to change?
- What will be different in the future?
- Why is this important to you?
- What about this bothers/excites you so much?
- How does this resonate with your values/vision?
- What I am hearing you say you want is...

The goal is to have mutual clarity.

Incite – The objective in this step is to foster multiple perspectives of the topic being discussed. Coaches help the Leader identify any support or obstacles, and analyze possible options. The pros and cons of each opportunity are evaluated to proactively prepare for and drive a commitment to act.

Now that the vision for the Leader's situation is clear, it is time to analyze different options or perspectives. Think of this step as the proverbial "brainstorming" phase of problem-solving to be followed by a discussion of the pros and cons of each option. Remember that coaching is moving a Leader toward action, and the purpose of this step is to incite some action!

The *Incite* step is also a time to consider other ways of looking at the issue – perhaps from another individual's point of view or shifting one's paradigm from negative to the positive. In the previous step, we learned that the Leader is struggling to provide difficult feedback to a peer. The continued dialogue may go like this ...

Coach: *"What are your options here? What can you do?"*

Leader: *"Well, I could do nothing."*

Coach: *"What are the upsides of that option?"*

Leader: *"I don't have to deal with it now ... I kind of like that, to be honest. It's what I am used to and it's my natural style so it's comfortable and it sure is efficient!"*

Coach: *"What are the downsides?"*

Leader: *"It's avoiding the issue. I will continue to alienate my team and the perception won't change."*

Coach: *"What else could you do?"*

Leader: *"I can 'bite my tongue' when I really want to interrupt someone!"*

Coach: *"What are the upsides of that option?"*

Leader: *"It allows people to continue with their ideas, and I don't come across as shutting them down."*

Coach: *"What are the downsides?"*

Leader: *"It can feel like a waste of time, but really, it is what I need to do."*

Coach: *"What else could you do?"*

Leader: *"I could ask that everyone prepare their ideas and be prepared to share – briefly – in the meeting."*

Coach: *"What are the upsides of that option?"*

> Leader: *"It forces all of us to share and engage, and it addresses my concern about wasting time because I can tell them they each get two minutes!"*
>
> Coach: *"Do you see any downsides to this option?"*
>
> Leader: *"The meeting could get long. I guess I would need to stress the two-minute limit."*
>
> Coach: *"What else could you do? ..."*

You get the idea. The purpose of *Incite* is to get the Leader to come up with potential options and to evaluate the upsides and downsides of each option. We have often found that simply asking for more options generates solutions that both the Coach and Leader had not previously considered. Frequently, it is one of these ideas that ultimately become the solution that works best.

> "My Coach is a guiding light for me in navigating my career. She puts aside her personal agenda and helps me to discover my own answers to perplexing organizational and career questions. She trusts in my abilities and has enabled me to trust myself more."

Incite is also useful in gaining perspective on perceived obstacles. For example, a Leader may be considering a new role, but is only focusing on the obstacles rather than the upsides of the change. The Coach can ask questions that foster a different perspective such as, *"What are the motivations for looking at a new role?"* or, *"What are the possible upsides or gains from a new opportunity?"* These questions incite the Leader to consider a different perspective and likely inspire the motivation to move toward a resolution.

Remember, *Incite* is all about perspectives and possibilities. The objective of *Incite* is to facilitate the Leader in generating multiple perspectives and creative approaches to resolve the perceived issue at hand.

Objective:

To facilitate the Leader in generating multiple perspectives and creative approaches.

Possible Questions:

- What has gotten in the way up to now?
- What are the opportunities for you (growth, challenge, stretch, accomplishments)?
- What are all the options or potential paths available?
- That's one way to view it, what's another?
- What is the impact of that option? What about the other?
- What are the upsides of that? What about the other?
- What are the consequences of that? What about the other?

The goal is for the Coach to facilitate an exploration of perspectives and options.

Decide – In this step, the Coach facilitates the Leader to make a conscious choice about achieving their vision by clearing the obstacles, confirming buy-in, and guiding the Leader toward the necessary next steps.

As demonstrated in the previous dialogue, the next step is to assist the Leader to make a decision or choose a path that works best for them. The Coach recaps the options and asks the Leader to make a choice. The Coach reminds the Leader of his long-term goals, and also supports the Leader in making plans for achieving those goals.

Coach: *"We have discussed several things you could do. Which action feels right?"*

Leader: *"Actually, I can do all of them. I really want to change this perception and many of these things are simple changes."*

Coach: *"And they definitely address your development area, don't they?"*

Leader: *"Yes, they certainly do. This will actually be a good experience for me."*

Coach: *"It certainly will, and I think it's great that you are taking a step to practice addressing it. OK ... so you are going to practice hearing people out and not interrupting! You are also going to ask everyone to prepare their ideas and share them at the next meeting."*

Leader: *"Yes!"*

Coach: *"When can you do that?"*

Leader: *"I have a meeting with the team tomorrow actually. I can do it then ... the sooner the better."*

Coach: *"Great. I'd love to hear how it goes. Will you come by after your meeting and let me know how it went?"*

Leader: *"Yes, definitely."*

"My Coach recognizes my strengths and the value I bring to the company. She has empowered me to own my strengths and value, as opposed to my tendency to focus on my deficits. This has allowed me to have a more balanced picture of myself and has enabled me to identify my personal brand and articulate it others inside and outside of the organization."

Oftentimes, Leaders may need some help in planning the next step. As we will discuss in Chapter 5, the key for the Coach is not to "take any monkeys" on their back. That is to say, not take the action items themselves, but to drive accountability with the Leader. Effective Coaches ask the right questions to get the Leader to deliberate their options and ultimately commit to all the necessary steps to achieve their desired outcomes. Effective Coaches do not leave a coaching session with their own list of action items and to-do's based on their conversation with the Leader. This is not about picking up the slack and adding commitments to your own agenda.

Remember, *Decide* is all about facilitating forward momentum. The objective is to facilitate your Leader to make a conscious choice, confirm their commitment, and determine the next steps toward the ultimate goal.

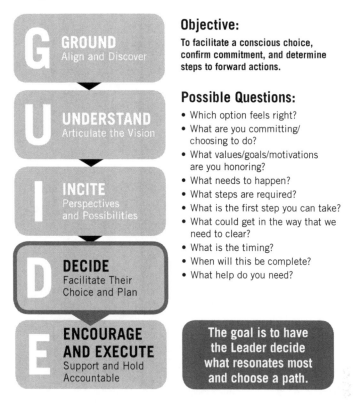

Objective:
To facilitate a conscious choice, confirm commitment, and determine steps to forward actions.

Possible Questions:
- Which option feels right?
- What are you committing/ choosing to do?
- What values/goals/motivations are you honoring?
- What needs to happen?
- What steps are required?
- What is the first step you can take?
- What could get in the way that we need to clear?
- What is the timing?
- When will this be complete?
- What help do you need?

The goal is to have the Leader decide what resonates most and choose a path.

Encourage and Execute – As a final step, the Coach *Encourages* the Leader to build upon the commitments made. The Coach builds confidence, provides encouragement, drives accountability, and generally acts as a champion. This ensures the coaching session ends with positive momentum in place and creates an expectation for a follow-up session. Remember, coaching is a process (particularly if it involves behavior change), and not a one-time event.

This is a critical, yet simple, step and includes supportive comments, as well as acknowledgement of the Leader. It is an ideal time to remind the Leader of their aspirations, the values they are honoring, the difficulties or challenges they are addressing, etc. In effect, this step ties it altogether and ensures the Leader feels that you have listened and you are supporting them.

Back to our example. The dialogue may go like this:

Coach:	*"I know it may be difficult to flex your style. However, I know you can do this, and I know you will benefit from this challenge."*
Leader:	*"Thanks so much. This has been very helpful. I appreciate your input. You always give such great advice."*
Coach:	*"I really want to hear how it goes! Will you stop by after you have had your meeting and let me know how it went?"*
Leader:	*"Absolutely. I would really like to debrief it when I am done."*

No, it was not advice! But, you have definitely helped them come up with the solution that works for THEM ... after all, it was their solution and they own it!

Remember, the objective of this final step in GUIDE Coaching is to *Encourage and Execute.* As the Coach, you want to have your Leader articulate her commitment with confidence around the decided course of action. Your role is to be her champion and encourage her to move forward.

Objective:

To articulate commitment, build confidence, and determine next coaching steps.

Possible Questions:

- How committed are you to do this?
- When will this be done and how will I know?
- I am eager to hear how it goes...
- I know you can do this... I am confident you will.
- When will we meet again?
- What will we discuss/revisit?
- Let's recap...

The goal is to guide the Leader forward and hold them accountable for their commitment!

GUIDE Coaching In Practice

GUIDE Coaching can feel awkward at first and may be uncomfortable for some Leaders to put into action – it is that "habit changing and expectation shifting" predicament again. We assure you, the process works. Once you implement it, you will see that there is flexibility to still be yourself, draw from your experience, and apply your knowledge (give advice, that is) as appropriate.

We repeatedly find ourselves coaching the "super individual contributor" or "Über IC." That is what we call Leaders who have been very successful as individuals within their businesses. These people have been rewarded for their productivity and their ability to execute, and who have been promoted into larger roles with larger spheres of influence. Instead of learning the art of how to influence and delegate to get things done, they still try to do it all themselves. It's a vicious cycle.

> "I was skeptical about being able to 'peer coach' when I didn't have a detailed knowledge of the topic, but I now understand it really is all about active listening and asking good questions vs. always feeling like I have to have the answer or have knowledge and experience in a particular area."

A fundamental premise of GUIDE Coaching, and one which you will hear us repeatedly emphasize, is the idea that you need to *be the guide on the side, not the sage on the stage.* Effective Coaches know how to facilitate problem solving, not solve the problem for others. This is a tough shift for many Leaders because it is typically how they ascended in their organization. They were good at solving problems, getting things done, being productive — and they were recognized and promoted because of it.

However, in our experience, Leaders that are effective at getting things done through others have a greater capacity for broader influence. You simply cannot continue to take on more tasks, expect to get it all done yourself, and be the one who always has the answers. At some point, there are not enough hours in the day. At some point, you have to teach others to think through their issues and solve them on their own. Coaching is a way of teaching others to find the answers that work for them.

Successful Leaders also apply the principles of GUIDE Coaching when they have to give someone feedback. Typically, delivering feedback (hopefully, specific in nature because it comes from focusing on observable behaviors) and clarifying the impact of those behaviors has a Leader in "telling" mode. It is very appropriate and effective to switch to "coaching" mode by asking the person questions, as opposed to automatically telling them what they need to do differently. Can you imagine the different tone that a conversation takes when a person is asked to come up with better ways to do something rather than being told what to do?

Here are some questions you can use to change a feedback conversation to become a more robust coaching dialogue:

- *"What do you make of this feedback?"*

- *"Are you surprised by it?"*

- *"What's your biggest take-away?"*

- *"How do you think you can go about addressing this?"*

- *"What might you do differently next time?"*

You are no longer just telling them how to address the feedback (and, admit it, selfishly feeling relieved because that conversation is over!). You are engaging in a dialogue designed to ensure true understanding. Remember, having them "own" the feedback and generating their own solutions creates stronger buy-in, increases the likelihood that the resulting behavior will change, and empowers them in the process!

"Sometimes we learn the hard way that it doesn't pay to get discouraged. Positive thinking is an intellectual choice, and by keeping our eyes focused on the light of optimism, we can restore faith in ourselves and stay clear of the shadows."

Chapter 5
The Art and Skill
of Coaching

"Always choose the path that moves in the direction of your dreams. Though your journey may be filled with many winding roads, when you are inspired to follow your dreams, you eventually find success, and discover it is less about the destination and more about the manner in which you traveled."

We have introduced you to the GUIDE Coaching process and the five-steps: *Ground, Understand, Incite, Decide, Encourage and Execute.*

We will now shift gears and examine the art and skill of coaching. It begins with the *"Leader's Vision"* at the center. That Vision is surrounded by the three principles of *Fulfillment, Values* and *Context.* Lastly, these three principles are embraced by the *"Spectrum of Eight"* skills that provide the push and pull of your coaching style.

The Model Overview: The Leader's Vision At The Center

GUIDE Coaching is an exercise in the art of balance. We have explained the process, and before we get into the skills required for effective coaching, we must first explain the GUIDE Coaching Model, which will clarify the fundamentals and provide the context to enable you to be most effective at coaching.

The GUIDE Coaching Model is a compass because strong Coaches are guides. The compass symbolizes our belief that, as a Coach, you need to understand the "destination" or the Leader's desired outcome to effectively coach them. Your Leaders are on a journey, and it is your role to guide them toward their desired destination or outcome. We call their destination or their desired outcome the *"Leader's Vision,"* and it is in the center of our model (and the center of the compass) because it should always be the anchor, the "hook," or the direction to which all their decisions and actions point.

Have you ever gone on a tour with a personal guide in the outdoors or in a new city? One of the first questions they will ask is, *"Where do you want to go?"* In other words, they want to understand your desired outcome or your goals and overall objectives of the tour. In turn, you do not expect them to judge your objectives (although they may very well have an opinion and you may very well ask it, but we will get to that later!). You do expect them to guide you through the unknown territory based on their experience and their knowledge. Their expertise is the territory and the route; it is their job to guide you through to your ultimate objectives. They use the necessary tools to navigate you through the experience.

Such is GUIDE Coaching: you are helping your Leader navigate through the territory to arrive at their destination or move closer to their goals and objectives.

The 3 Principles: Values, Fulfillment and Context

The GUIDE Coaching compass is built around the Leader's Vision because that is the center of all the activity and decisions. The Leader's Vision should always be the anchor, or the litmus test, of their decisions and actions. Also surrounding the Leader's Vision are three key principles that help you, and them, gain a deeper understanding of their vision and the specifics of their situation. These are essentially those factors that impact the Leader on a consistent basis. The three principles are *Values, Fulfillment* and *Context*.

Holding Others Accountable

Giving Advice

Genuinely Interested

Driving Conscious Choice

Fostering Perspectives

Catalyst for Action

Listening and Intuition

Collaboration

Fulfillment

LEADER'S VISION

Values

Context

Coaching is an art of balance more than a prescriptive science.

Values

The first principle is the Leader's *Values*. In other words, what is most important to the Leader, and what "guides" their decisions and choices? Much of this information or context about those you coach comes through in the *Ground* step of GUIDE Coaching, and it is why we emphasize how critically important this step is in the coaching relationship. By understanding what your Leader *Values*, you can then help GUIDE him toward making choices and decisions that are consistent with what he believes is important to him. *Values* can conflict and differ from person to person and, here is a real predicament: they can change! This is the crux of why understanding them and revisiting them often is so important.

Have you thought about your own values and what drives how you spend your day, week, year, or life? Would your spouse, significant other, family, friends, peers, managers, direct reports and other colleagues agree that these are your values? How do they know? Can you venture to guess the values of your friends, family and co-workers? How do you know?

Take a moment to explore your values and what is important to you by completing the *"Values Sorting Exercise."* First, read the definitions for the values provided and assign a numerical ranking in the box to the left of the definition that describes your "Ideal Values." By "Ideal," we mean those values that mean the most to you, and that you most cherish.

Next, assign a numerical ranking using the box to the right of the definition to describe your "Actual Values." Be honest. This ranking will most likely be different and will be reflective of how your behaviors and your priorities indicate you are actually prioritizing your values as demonstrated by how you are living your life today.

Step One: Rank these 18 values by number in order of those most important to you ... your IDEAL Values!

Step Two: Now go back and reorder these values. Think about how others perceive your values according to how you are actually living (how you spend your time, money, and energy). Be realistic.

Ideal Ranking		Actual Ranking
☐ Challenge and Growth	Working on tasks and goals which stretch my skills and help me develop, grow and mature.	☐
☐ Community	Being involved with a group that has a larger purpose beyond myself. Being part of a team.	☐

Ideal Ranking		Actual Ranking
☐ Creativity	Being innovative and using my artistic or "out of the box" thinking. Creating new and better ways of doing things.	☐
☐ Enjoyment	Enjoying and having fun doing my job. Liking my work and the environment in which I work.	☐
☐ Expertise	Being an authority on what I do — becoming known and respected for my expertise.	☐
☐ Family	Having time to spend with my family or significant non-work relationships.	☐
☐ Friendship	Working with people I like and trust and being liked and trusted by them.	☐
☐ Health	Being physically and mentally fit.	☐
☐ Independence	Having control over how I spend my time and complete my work.	☐
☐ Leadership	Influencing others on the job. Creating visions which other people adopt, support and act on.	☐
☐ Location	Living in a specific geographic area or type of community.	☐
☐ Loyalty	Feeling I am part of an organization. Being committed to helping it achieve its goals.	☐
☐ Personal Achievement	Accomplishing important personal goals. Being involved in personally significant undertakings, whether or not they bring personal recognition from others.	☐
☐ Position/Power	Having formal control and authority over resources and decisions.	☐
☐ Recognition	Being seen by others as successful and important. Having my contributions valued and acknowledged by others.	☐
☐ Security	Having a stable job and secure employment.	☐
☐ Service	Contributing to the satisfaction and the well-being of others. Helping others and improving society.	☐
☐ Wealth	Having money and a high standard of living.	☐

We can form a clearer picture of our values by analyzing the choices we make and how we live our lives. Gandhi said, *"Action expresses priorities."* This is such a simple, yet profound statement, but it gets at the core of what we mean by values. We express our priorities by how we spend our time, money and resources. BUT ... is that what we would articulate? We find that while many Leaders believe they know their values, it isn't until they go through a process of values sorting that their actual priorities really become crystal clear. It is not an easy process, and it is often a frustrating exercise to "sort out" what we really believe we value in our lives.

We use the *"Values Sorting Exercise"* with many Leaders in our coaching partnerships, workshops and courses to help individuals understand their values. We use it as a tool with those learning to coach because it provides excellent insight into potential coaching biases.

The "ah-ha moments" that happen in the *"Values Sorting Exercise"* are often life changing and validating. When Leaders complete their "Ideal Values" sort, and then compare it to how they are living and behaving as shown by how their "Actual Values" are demonstrated, they frequently see a major disconnect. It is important to understand why these can be so vastly different and whether that is a potential source of confusion or conflict for an individual. Is this pointing to an issue? Or, is this indicative of a point of time in life? At points in life, it is not uncommon to feel compelled to make trade-offs regarding work and family and perhaps sacrifice in the short-term to honor a longer-term value.

Take Josh's experience in going through the *"Values Sorting Exercise."* He was alarmed and concerned when he compared his top five ideal values with his top five actual values in terms of how he was living his life.

Ideal Values	Actual Values
1. Family	1. Position/Power
2. Health	2. Recognition
3. Friendship	3. Expertise
4. Enjoyment	4. Challenge and Growth
5. Independence	5. Wealth

At first look, you may be alarmed at the difference and assume that Josh is not living an authentic life or that he is significantly off-course. Now, consider that Josh was a newlywed, early in his career with just five years at his company, and pursuing his MBA. He was working about 60 hours a week as a new Sales Manager, while going to school in the evenings and on weekends. After discussing his values, Josh acknowledged that while he felt stretched, tired, and a bit out of shape, he recognized that this current state was a "trade-off" in the pursuit of his life and career ambitions.

While he wished he had more time to spend with his new bride, they both recognized that his two-year commitment to obtain his MBA was a necessary investment of his time and their resources to facilitate the achievement of his career goal to become a Vice President. Furthermore, the education and focus on his career at the present time would ultimately help him fulfill their financial goals and desires to start a family in a few years. There was logic in why his actual and ideal values differed. It was a trade-off at a specific time in his life, and Josh appreciated the validation that his current state was worth the pursuit of achieving his ideal values. In fact, it motivated him to persevere and do well to achieve success in his MBA and in his current role.

"People take different roads seeking fulfillment and happiness. Just because they aren't on your road doesn't mean they've gotten lost."
-Dalai Lama

Understanding what is important to your Leader goes a long way in understanding what drives them, what motivates them, and ultimately what choices and decisions they make for the short-term and the long-term. Your role as a Coach is to help your Leaders understand and articulate their values in the beginning of the coaching partnership to serve as an anchor and a compass in their decisions and actions.

Fulfillment

The second principle is *Fulfillment*. In other words, *"What fulfills or satisfies the Leader?"* As in the *Values* step, understanding what fulfills, satisfies or motivates your Leaders helps you guide them toward their long-term objectives. To understand this, we ask questions like this:

- *"What do you find personally fulfilling?"*

- *"What do you most look forward to everyday?"*

- *"If you didn't come to work here, what would you choose to do?"*

- *"What is the highlight of your day?"*

- *"We are at your retirement party and toasting your career, what do you want people to say about you?"*

Consider Susan. She was moving up the corporate ladder at a quick pace and was offered all sorts of extra assignments and opportunities that added to her reputation for stellar performance. She was gaining frequent exposure in the organization and was clearly being groomed for a more senior role. When working with her Coach, there was a sense that Susan felt unfulfilled. She knew she should be thrilled at how her career was progressing, yet she felt as if something was missing.

Consider asking: *"Susan, what gets you up and going every day? What is the highlight of your week?"*

By asking just a few key questions designed to address the second principle of *Fulfillment*, it became very clear that while Susan enjoyed moving up the corporate ladder, she also had a strong desire to give back to her community through her volunteer work. She found that she had less time available as she began to work more hours. Eventually, her norm was to sacrifice the hours she dedicated to volunteering within her community and serving on the local school advisory board for more hours spent at work. She could not articulate when or how this all happened, but she realized that the shift was now her reality. In fact, this led to her current unfulfilled state.

Fortunately for Susan, being able to identify that which fulfilled her – giving back within her community – allowed her to come up with a solution that worked really well for all involved. She suggested to her senior leadership team that she begin to play a larger role in the community representing the company on various boards

> "My Coach makes it easy. Having a Coach by my side, encouraging me, and making me reflect on myself has been a tremendous value."

and spearheaded a mentor/mentee program in the local school system. The company loved having such a visible and successful face in the community, and Susan loved being able to feel fulfilled while at work. It was a win/win!

Understanding what is personally fulfilling to your Leader goes a long way toward helping them to figure out why they might not be feeling completely satisfied. Many Leaders say that in the view of their peers they should feel great, but for some reason, they have a tiny voice inside their head whispering, *"I know I should be thrilled, but ...."*

A Leader who worked in Account Management landed an exclusive deal. Her peers were thrilled for her, and frankly a bit jealous. She had managed to land a huge account that would keep her working (and keep paying off) for a long time. Yet, the Leader did not share their same level of enthusiasm. She knew she should be happy, yet she still felt as though there was a little voice whispering that something was missing. The principle of *Fulfillment* helps to identify what that voice is saying!

Context

The third principle is *Context*. A client of ours, Bob Cancalosi, Chief Learning Officer at GE Healthcare, once stated, *"Content is King, Context is the Kingdom, and Connectedness is the World."* Light bulbs went off with this statement! Context really does put perspective on a situation. The definition of context from the *American Heritage Dictionary* is, *"1. The part of a written or spoken statement in which a word or passage at issue occurs; that which leads up to and follows and often specifies the meaning of a particular expression. 2. The circumstances in which a particular event occurs; a situation."*

Context is understanding your Leader's circumstances from both internal and external perspectives. From the internal perspective, it is understanding their readiness for being coached. From an external perspective, it is understanding what is going on around them, such as their environment, their company, or the impact of other people who may influence their circumstances.

Recognizing the value of internal perspective is vital. We would like to believe that most people are ready and willing to be coached. And, now that you know "how" to coach and understand the benefits of being coached, it seems everyone would want to experience coaching. However, the reality is that many of those we work with would benefit from coaching, but for one reason or another, they are simply not willing or are not ready. In our experience, there are three key factors to determine whether an individual is ready to be coached. We call these the *"Factors for Coaching Readiness."*

• Introspective – "Self Aware"

Potential Leaders must first be self-aware or introspective, and be motivated to understand how their behaviors are perceived by others in the workplace. If they are not interested or able to show some vulnerability (for example, not knowing everything or not being perfect), the best Coaches in the world will not be able to uncover the "hook" which propels the Leader to "care," much less move forward.

• Invested – "Owns It"

Some potential Leaders are very aware of how they are perceived in the organization, but they either rationalize it (by saying things like, *"they just don't understand"* or *"they are all wrong"*) and play the victim, or expect others (typically their boss) to "fix" the situation. Potential Leaders need to accept the fact that it is their job to address whatever they want to change. The proverbial "monkey" is on their back and no one else's. Their success in achieving their future goals depends on the person in the mirror looking back at them.

• Inspired – "Motivated to Act"

Even if there is personal ownership of whatever the issue is, there needs to be a willingness or motivation for the potential Leader to move out of their comfort zone (which is a very comfortable, safe place to be!). They must take some personal risk, and challenge themselves to take those first scary steps forward. We refer to this as the "hook" – the "what's in it for the Leader" – to begin to make significant change.

You are likely already assessing individuals with whom you work regarding their "readiness" for coaching. We encourage you to not jump to conclusions without sitting down with them first and asking the key questions found in the *Grounding* and *Understanding* steps of GUIDE Coaching. The goal is to avoid either "writing people off" because of their current performance or behavior, or assuming others do not need or want coaching because they are "superstars."

While anyone can coach anyone (you can coach not only your team members, but your peers, your boss, or folks outside of work, even your kids!), individuals have to WANT to be coached. In other words, the old adage holds true: *"You can lead a horse to water, but you can't make him drink."* At the end of the day, the Leader is the one doing the work (or not). Your role as a Coach is to ensure that they understand the impact or consequences of doing nothing, not making a behavior change, or deciding not to move forward. After all, that, in and of itself, is a decision.

That does not mean to say that everyone will be a "willing Leader" initially. Yes, there will be some people who seek you out for advice (which you can then turn into coaching). There may even be some people who have had formal Coaches before and actually ask for you to coach them. However, there is another group of people who may not understand what coaching is or who are not aware that they need coaching. With this second group, you as the Coach would initiate the coaching, typically by providing specifics on behavioral feedback that you have observed. And, even after that initial discussion, there will be people who choose not to be coached (again, it is their decision, as long as you have communicated the impact).

Good Leaders have many of the same attributes as good Coaches! Namely, they need to be life-long learners, genuinely interested in "being the best they can be." They also need to be humble, and be able to show their vulnerability. They need to be able to really get "the message behind the message." Leaders need to be reflective. They need to be open and willing to think about the tough questions (and sometimes the tougher answers!). They need to be able to look in the mirror and accept responsibility for what they can control and move themselves forward.

Next, we should consider the meaning of external context. By understanding the context of our Leader's external circumstances, you are able to best guide them towards making appropriate decisions that work with their situation. Furthermore, by having the Leader articulate their context, they gain clarity on their situation and have a better grasp of present circumstances. The old adage, *sometimes you have to step out of the frame to see the picture*" applies here. Frequently, your Leaders will be so immersed in their circumstance that they have lost perspective and fail to see the big picture for what it is and how it is impacting them. By facilitating a discussion to gain context, your Leaders gain greater clarity and are able to distance themselves momentarily to make a better decision. Without context, decisions are often made in a vacuum and without consideration for factors and people that will be impacted by the decisions.

As a Coach, it is best if you are able to help your Leader define and understand the context. That may be as simple as reminding the Leader to consider the context of the situation in order to make a more informed decision. If you are coaching your team members, peers or even Leaders with whom you have regular interaction, you may likely be more familiar with the context in which they are operating. As the Coach, you will be able to guide your Leader to consider all facets of the context – the positive and the negative!

> "My Coach is great at helping me to navigate difficult communications and complicated dynamics with my manager and with employees. She quickly grasps the situations and helps me find the right words to use to get my point across in a positive and reinforcing way."

Consider Seth. He was assessing whether to make a substantial career change within his company. Essentially, he was looking to move from a function where he was well-known and had a strong network of supporters and great visibility, to a different function where he essentially had no track record. He wanted to make this move to broaden his skill base and determine if his interest and skill in the area could positively impact his future career goals.

Seth's Coach asked him to consider the context of the situation. What else was going on within the organization that might facilitate or negate Seth's ability to make an informed decision? As it turns out, the company was facing some economic uncertainty due to some turbulent markets, and financial belts were being tightened across the company. For the first time in the history of the company, there were rumors that layoffs were being planned as a cost-cutting measure.

Upon considering the context of what was going on around him, Seth decided that now was not the right time to become "low man on the totem pole" or to become a virtual unknown in a function in which he did not have a tremendous amount of depth or experience. He decided to remain in his current function where he had a tremendous amount of visibility and support and "weather the storm." He knew he would have an opportunity in the future to consider the move again when the business was more stable.

Understanding the context of the situation allows us to make more sound decisions, rather than making decisions in a vacuum without all the facts!

The Push and Pull of GUIDE Coaching

The final part of the GUIDE Coaching Process is the *"Spectrum of Eight."* As you saw on the GUIDE Coaching compass, there are a *"Spectrum of Eight"* skills surrounding the *"Leader's Vision."* These *"Spectrum of Eight"* are, in effect, opposing skills (or complimentary, depending on your perspective) that constantly push and pull from one another. These skills demonstrate the delicate balance in what we call *"The Art of Coaching."*

Coaching is neither a science, nor is it all "black and white." There is a substantial amount of "gray" that requires Coaches to have a high level of comfort with ambiguity – or at least learn to appreciate ambiguity. Coaching is often more subjective than objective. There is not a right way or a wrong way to address each situation that arises, but rather a most effective approach for that moment and that situation. Staying flexible and being open to mid-course corrections is imperative. Effective coaching requires a constant balance between the push and pull of the skills along the spectrum.

Coaching is an art of balance
more than a prescriptive science.

The "Spectrum of Eight"

1. Genuinely Interested/Catalyst for Action

Effective Coaches are genuinely interested in their Leaders. They ask insightful questions and seek to understand the Leader, their values, what fulfills them, and the context of their circumstances. However, they must balance this genuine interest in their Leader with driving their Leader forward to make solid, sound decisions that lead to positive actions. In other words, effective Coaches do not get caught up in the story, the details, or the background. At some point, too much background information becomes irrelevant to moving them forward, and can become a distraction, or a crutch. As we discussed earlier, you want to show you care, but you do not want to enable your Leaders to dwell on their situation so it becomes therapy session. The role of a Coach is to care and to understand context, but to also drive the Leader to actions and decisions that keep them moving forward toward their vision!

2. Fostering Perspectives/Driving Conscious Choice

"Coaching provides a platform to have a different discussion — to sit back and think about how to approach things from a different perspective."

Effective Coaches are able to facilitate their Leaders through a process of understanding their situation from different perspectives or options. This eventually allows the Leader to determine the best viewpoint from which to assess their situation and/or the most appropriate route to pursue toward their desired outcome. As Coaches, your role is to help the Leader evaluate their situation from many angles to gain clarity on the situation. However, this process cannot go on forever, or you will both be "lost in the forest" of details and over-analysis. The ultimate goal is to drive them forward to making a conscious, well-thought-out, and carefully evaluated choice.

On the flip side, if the Coach gets too laser-focused on an outcome or gaining commitment to an action, there may be missed opportunities to evaluate varying perspectives or to consider alternative, more impactful options. This frequently prohibits you from truly discovering and understanding "what's below the surface" or exploring potential options. Again, there is a balance in doing this as a Coach. Effective Coaches do not get caught up in exhausting the process of over-analyzing the options. Yet, if you do not facilitate the Leader in considering different perspectives, they may miss what is really important: the opportunity to consider the full context of the situation, or to identify potential "out of the box" (or out of their comfort zone) solutions.

3. Listening and Intuition/Giving Advice

Effective Coaches are excellent listeners, both of the spoken and the unspoken message (e.g., that which is conveyed by your Leader's non-verbal cues). Effective Coaches also know themselves well enough to self-manage

> "If you don't mind, I'd like to stop listening to you and start talking."

their biases and individual experiences, so as not to inadvertently influence the Leader's decisions inappropriately by giving advice. If you are naturally directive, you may need to manage your tendency to give advice and your desire to "tell" your Leader what to do based upon your own experience.

On the other hand, as a Coach, you must be able to listen to your Leader, read between the proverbial lines, and sometimes state the obvious! For example, if it sounds like the Leader is complaining, whining and avoiding the issue, it is often very effective for the Coach to state what they are observing: *It sounds to me like you are avoiding this issue and trying to take the easy way out by not confronting it.* The Leader has every right to confirm or refute this statement. Remember, it is not about you being "right," but rather it is about using your intuition to prompt further learning by your Leader. This can be a very effective tool for moving them forward. Again, it is a balance and an art. Everyone's coaching style will look and feel different, but the ability to actively listen while managing a tendency to "tell" or "have the answer" is a skill we see Leaders and Coaches grapple with continuously.

4. Collaboration/Holding Others Accountable

Effective Coaches are able to balance the fine line of collaboration with their Leader. On the one hand, you want there to be a sense of, "we're in this together" so that there is trust, and a sense that you truly care about their success. But, it is also incredibly important to realize that the role of the Coach is to hold

> "My Coach keeps me focused on what I need to work on."

the Leader accountable for their decisions and their actions, not to take on those decisions or actions as your own.

This point is important – and frequently a very powerful concept to Leaders learning GUIDE Coaching! The idea that as Coaches you should not be taking on action items for your Leader's decisions or issues is tremendously liberating. You should be empowering your Leader to own their actions and their outcomes.

How many times has someone come to your office with an issue and by the time they have left, you have signed up for a list of action items to complete in pursuit of solving their issue? That is not GUIDE Coaching. That is, in fact, taking on their issue. We call this phenomenon "taking their monkeys on your back." In coaching, it is "their monkey," so they are accountable. Your role is to be a strong partner in the process by asking the right questions, supporting your Leader, and caring enough to guide them toward decisions or actions. Your role is to move them forward when they are stuck or processing information for the right decision. Your role is not to take on actions to solve their problems.

The *"Art of Balance"* chart shows what can happen when the balance of positive coaching behaviors or skills gets skewed in one direction or the other. The artful balance of being both genuinely interested and being a catalyst for action goes off track if you are too interested as a Coach and spend too much time gathering information. On the other hand, if you are too much of a catalyst for action, you may focus on the "fix" to the detriment of gaining some pertinent information.

Watch-out	Complementary Behaviors		Watch-out
Too Much Information	**Genuinely Interested** Demonstrating Curiosity Leading to Discovery Building Relationships Building Trust	**Catalyst for Action** Gaining Commitment to Actions Driving Progress Achieving Results and Focusing on Metrics	Focus on the Fix

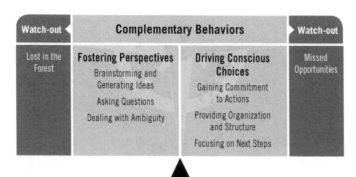

Watch-out	Complementary Behaviors		Watch-out
Lost in the Forest	**Fostering Perspectives** Brainstorming and Generating Ideas Asking Questions Dealing with Ambiguity	**Driving Conscious Choices** Gaining Commitment to Actions Providing Organization and Structure Focusing on Next Steps	Missed Opportunities

Watch-out	Complementary Behaviors		Watch-out
Therapy	**Listening and Intuition** Reading Body Language Reading "Between the Lines" Showing Empathy	**Giving Advice** Leveraging Experience Moving the Leader Forward Driving Actions and Conclusions	Too Directive

Watch-out	Complementary Behaviors		Watch-out
Taking Their Monkeys	**Collaboration** Demonstrating Care and Concern Supporting and Championing Desiring to Assist	**Holding Others Accountable** Gaining Commitment to Actions Managing Separation of Self and Leader Limiting Rationalizations	Disengaged

Bringing It All Together

Our philosophy is that anyone can be a Coach and that anyone can be coached. There is no requirement for any expertise on the subject area. Rather, there is an expectation that the Coach will ask the right questions and drive the right dialogue to guide the person being coached – the Leader – to the correct personal decision.

We mentioned earlier that GUIDE Coaching is a process that is linear in theory, yet ambiguous in practice. With this in mind, it should now be obvious that you will not need to address the *Ground* step in every coaching session. But, what about the other steps? Do you need to go through the entire process each time you meet with your Leader? The answer is … it depends! It depends on the topic and the situation.

In practice, you may go through all the steps in one session if the topic is one that allows for it. For some narrow topics that are focused on the resolution of a specific issue, the session may easily lend itself to quickly going through each step in one coaching conversation.

The examples we have used throughout this book have predominantly been focused on simple, narrow topics that lend themselves to easily following the process through its entirety in one session. However, for much broader topics, such as major career decisions, career development, or life choices, the Leader may need time to process and go through certain steps between sessions. In such scenarios, there may still be action items, but they are in pursuit of completing certain steps in the GUIDE Coaching process.

For example, let's take the scenario of the Leader who is considering multiple job offers, one of which requires relocation of him and his family:

Leader: *"Thanks for meeting with me. I really need some advice."*
Coach: *"Sure …"*

Leader: *"I have a big decision to make in the next week or so. I've been offered two jobs in the sales organization."*

Coach: *"That's fantastic. Congratulations!"*

Leader: *"Thanks … but it's not that simple. Both opportunities are very different and I'm having a hard time making a decision. One is here in Atlanta working for a Leader I really admire and have wanted to work with for a long time. The other is a great role in Beijing … an international role that would really stretch and challenge me."*

Coach: *"Sounds like a great problem to have. Tell me more about what you are deciding."*

Leader: *"My decision is really around what is best for my career. I know I would learn so much from Ilene, and she is known for her passion for developing others. And, that role is more internally focused, which is an experience I need. The Beijing role is a sales role, externally focused, that I could technically do in my sleep."*

Coach: *"I see. What else do you need to know to make your decision?"*

Leader: *"I need to talk to each manager and find out their expectations, metrics, etc. of the role."*

Coach: *"So what do you need to do next?"*

Leader: *"I need to set up some time with each manager and get my questions answered."*

Coach: *"Of course. When can you do that?"*

Leader: *"I'll do that this afternoon. Can I come back to you after I have more information?"*

Coach: *"Absolutely. I would also ask that you think about your vision for your career. Think about and let's discuss what you want to achieve in the next few years and how each role either helps or doesn't help you move toward that vision."*

> Leader: *"Yes, that's such a great point. I can do that. Great, thanks for your advice."*

This second example has more complexity than the first one, as it is a broader topic that cannot be worked through in one session. The Leader clearly needs time to gather more information, process his situation, and consider the upsides and downsides of each option. In the next meeting, the Coach and Leader would continue through the GUIDE Coaching process.

In this case, the Coach and Leader spent some time in the *Understand* step to revisit the Leader's vision to align the Leader on the criteria for his desired outcome. Going through the *Understand* step got the Leader motivated and excited that, whichever job he accepted, it was moving him toward his vision for career fulfillment. The Coach then moved into the *Incite* step. Notice that the Coach asked the Leader to work through the *Incite* step as their "homework" – their action item – for their next session. The Coach can prompt this step to begin the process of going through the pros and cons of each option, but it is too broad of a topic to be resolved in that one session. The Coach, in fact, went through all of the steps of GUIDE Coaching: there are action items, and a date when they will meet again to further discuss the situation. At the next session, they can pick up from where they left off, but the Leader will have done much of the exploring on his own and now requires the Coach to help process his final decision.

"Excellence is never an accident; it is always the result of high intention, sincere effort, intelligent direction, skillful execution and the vision to see obstacles as opportunities."

Chapter 6
Where are You as a Coach?

"There are many things in life that will capture your eye. But very few will capture your heart. These are the ones to pursue. These are the ones worth keeping."

You have probably started to think about the areas in which you might excel and where you might struggle as a Coach. In our experience, the most effective Leaders and Coaches are those that are the most self-aware: they know what they are good at, and they know where they need to adapt to achieve desired results and influence others. It is the same premise with GUIDE Coaching! The most effective Coaches are those that are willing to stretch themselves as they try new approaches to motivating others (and themselves). Strong Coaches remember the *Values* exercise (or something like it!) and do not infuse their own values on others. Strong Coaches are, most importantly, sincere and authentic.

We believe that self-awareness comes from many sources, including your own self-assessment, feedback from others, and personality or leadership style instruments. When combined, these sources of feedback provide a 360° perspective of how you are viewed and offer valuable insight into your strengths and gaps. The key is that it must be put into context to become personally meaningful.

As we said, GUIDE Coaching is an art of balance more than a prescriptive science. Remember the *"Art of Balance"* chart from the last chapter? It highlights the *"Spectrum of Eight"* behaviors a Coach may have and shows what that behavior looks like when taken to excess on either end.

1. Self assessment

We are confident that you have had a few opportunities throughout your experience to have an idea of your style, strengths, and areas that are "outside of your comfort zone." We affectionately call these your gaps or your "watch-outs." Simply put, these are areas that either do not come as naturally to you or that you have not developed into a strength. We all have them, and, in our experience, no one ever "arrives" as a Leader, especially if one wants to continue to grow and adapt to the inevitable changes around them to continue to be effective.

Referring back to the *"Art of Balance"* in the GUIDE Coaching Model, you can assess yourself on where you fall along the spectrum required for effective GUIDE Coaching. You will notice that your "comfort zone" is likely where your strengths lie, while the "watch-outs" are the cautions of overusing that strength. You may need to stretch, develop, or be cognizant of these "watch-outs" in order to adapt your behavior.

Rate yourself on where you fall. The pivot point at the center represents a good balance between the two behaviors. If you believe you have a good balance between the two, you would simply indicate that balance by marking the continuum. As you evaluate the additional behaviors on either side of the center pivot, you are indicating where you feel your balance may "tip" in one direction or the other. Again, you can mark that spot on the continuum. This is helpful to know as you begin to understand what strengths you bring, and what you need to watch out for when coaching.

Watch-out	Complementary Behaviors		Watch-out
Too Much Information	**Genuinely Interested** Demonstrating Curiosity Leading to Discovery Building Relationships Building Trust	**Catalyst for Action** Gaining Commitment to Actions Driving Progress Achieving Results and Focusing on Metrics	Focus on the Fix

▲

Watch-out	Complementary Behaviors		Watch-out
Lost in the Forest	**Fostering Perspectives** Brainstorming and Generating Ideas Asking Questions Dealing with Ambiguity	**Driving Conscious Choices** Gaining Commitment to Actions Providing Organization and Structure Focusing on Next Steps	Missed Opportunities

▲

Watch-out	Complementary Behaviors		Watch-out
Therapy	**Listening and Intuition** Reading Body Language Reading "Between the Lines" Showing Empathy	**Giving Advice** Leveraging Experience Moving the Leader Forward Driving Actions and Conclusions	Too Directive

▲

Watch-out	Complementary Behaviors		Watch-out
Taking Their Monkeys	**Collaboration** Demonstrating Care and Concern Supporting and Championing Desiring to Assist	**Holding Others Accountable** Gaining Commitment to Actions Managing Separation of Self and Leader Limiting Rationalizations	Disengaged

▲

2. Feedback from Others

Another excellent source of awareness of one's strengths and gaps in coaching is feedback from those who know you and interact with you regularly at work. Our coaching practice is built around the belief that the way a Leader is perceived directly impacts their ability to influence others and get things done through others. The most effective Leaders and Coaches are perceived as adaptable in their style and approach, depending on the individual and the situation. Unfortunately, we have learned that one style does not fit all. So it is with coaching and it begins with an awareness of how you are perceived. We are not saying that you have to be a chameleon, nor that you need to deviate completely from your strengths, but knowing when situations require a varied approach or stretching outside your comfort zone is extremely effective. There are skills in coaching that will not suit everyone's style and strengths.

> "My Coach enables me to see my strengths and abilities ... by highlighting them in a way that allows me to own them and represent them in a way that moves me forward."

If you are unsure of what the perception is about how you influence and get things done, just ask!

- *"What do you perceive as my most unique and effective strengths as a Leader or a Coach?"*

- *"What do you perceive are the areas in which I could be more effective as a Leader or a Coach?"*

- *"Is my style more directive or facilitative?"*

- *"Is my style more creative or structured?"*

- *"Am I perceived as genuinely interested in others or more focused on the result or task at hand?"*

- *"Am I perceived as a good listener, or do I tend to give more advice?"*

- *"Am I perceived as more of a 'doer' or someone that lets others do?"*

- *"Am I perceived as more creative or detail-oriented?"*

- *"Am I perceived as more collaborative or more driven to hold others accountable?"*

Asking these questions of those with whom you work will certainly provide some feedback and insight as to how you are thought of within the organization across the *"Spectrum of Eight."*

3. Personality or Style Instruments

We have used many personality and leadership style instruments in our consulting practice. We believe that all of them tend to provide valuable insight and information about your style, strengths, potential gaps, tendencies, etc. If you have access to such instruments, by all means take advantage of the opportunity to learn more about yourself. These instruments are objective tools that can help us to better understand ourselves from the inside-out and provide a simple medium and a common language with which to describe our personalities.

We are familiar with the *Herrmann Brain Dominance Instrument (HBDI),* the *Birkman Profile, DiSC, Insights Colors, Myers-Briggs,* the *Hogan,* and several other instruments. We have found that while each is unique, they typically provide consistent information about your leadership and coaching style. We are not going to endorse any specific instrument, nor are we going to explain each of these instruments. However, we are going to introduce a concept around GUIDE Coaching styles as related to our GUIDE Coaching model.

In 460 BC, Hippocrates identified four different temperaments of human beings. Plato followed this idea and reaffirmed his belief in four different types of people in 428 BC. Many great thinkers around the world have continued to expand upon this idea through the years such that today it is a widely-held belief that, *"You can put all the people in the world into one of four categories and accurately describe how they will behave."*

Most of the style instruments on the market are based on this theory, and the output and ultimate take-away from them is a description of one's style or approach to problem solving and thinking. For simplicity, we have summarized what we see as four different coaching styles based upon the GUIDE Coaching Model. You can literally plot your tendencies along the *"Spectrum of Eight"* skills to determine your primary coaching style. Once you have an idea of your primary coaching style, you can review your potential strengths and cautions as a Coach. In our experience, individuals tend to identify with one or two of the styles.

For example, let's say that Jo reviews the *"Spectrum of Eight"* on the previous page and reflects that based on her own self-assessment and feedback that she receives from others, she knows that she errs on the side of being a strong listener and very intuitive. She also is known for being very collaborative. Looking at the chart above, Jo would surmise that her GUIDE Coaching style would tend to be *Facilitative,* and founded upon being *"Connection-Oriented."*

Jo would recognize that this is her natural style, and one that brings a tremendous amount of strength to her ability to coach others. She is naturally empathetic, has a very caring approach, and holds a holistic view of each individual. She is sincerely interested in becoming involved with each Leader, genuinely listens to them, and truly desires to assist. All of these would be considered formidable strengths in a Coach, right? Absolutely! But, the strengths of each coaching style also bring some cautions as over-used strengths can become issues.

In this case, Jo needs to watch out for being too facilitative, which could result in accepting excuses and rationalizations from her Leader. Jo needs to ensure that she is not being too enabling of behaviors that need to change. She needs to watch out that she doesn't become too subjective, instead of giving merit to some of the facts at hand.

Using the chart on the next page, any Coach can take a look at their natural style to determine what strengths they bring to the coaching relationship, and where they need to be cautious of over-doing a good thing.

Goal-Oriented: Directive		Option-Oriented: Creative	
Strengths	**Cautions**	**Strengths**	**Cautions**
Objective/Fact-based	Too Direct	"Big Picture" Outlook	Lack Of Structure
Focused	"Fix It" vs. Understand	Creative Perspective	Lack Of Facts/Details
"To The Point"	Impersonal/Cold	Dealing with Ambiguity	Doesn't Hold Accountable
Metrics Focused	Not Helpful	Focus On The "Why?"	Too Hands-off
Doesn't Rationalize	Too Judgmental	Optimism	Listening

Process-Oriented: Structured		Connection-Oriented: Facilitative	
Strengths	**Cautions**	**Strengths**	**Cautions**
Thorough	"My Way" Is Only Way	Empathetic	Accepts Rationalizing
Organized	Too Hands-on	Caring Approach	Apologetic/Too Enabling
Structured	Too Much Structure	Holistic	Too Subjective vs. Facts
Focus On Next Steps	Too Prescriptive	Involving/Listening	Talking Too Much
Objective	Overwhelm With Details	Desire To Assist	"Giving In"

Where did you land? Is it clear where you fall on the chart? Are you cognizant of the strengths that you bring to being a Coach and the areas where you should practice caution?

"Excellence is the result of caring more than others think is wise, risking more than others think is safe, dreaming more than others think is practical, and expecting more than others think is possible."

Chapter 7
Coaching for Performance

"Change is life giving. It helps us to grow into someone greater than we already are."

When we initially began helping Leaders to become effective Coaches, our consulting engagement ended there (after, of course, observing them actually coaching and giving them feedback along the way!). Yet, Leaders kept asking us for advice on how they could go about helping to facilitate their Leaders' "plan of attack" in terms of moving forward (remember, as a Coach, you are not developing it for them!).

In our experience assessing Leaders around the world, we find that professional development (often measured in terms of observable behaviors) tends to fall into five categories:

Improvement: When people think of development, they most often think of taking steps to address a gap, either where there is a lack of knowledge, skills, or experience, or where a specific behavior is having an unintended negative impact. In this case, the focus is on "closing the gap" to bring

> "It is incredibly liberating to apply GUIDE Coaching and 'get the monkey off my back' in terms of owning other people's development. They really need to accept, own, and act on their constructive feedback, rather than having me do the work for them. I wondered why I was taking charge of so many actions for others on my team. GUIDE Coaching helped me to understand how to coach them and give them full accountability."

the attribute at least up to what is expected of someone at their level in the organization. Although this is the most traditional definition of development, we believe examining other approaches can further increase a Leader's effectiveness and likelihood of achieving their goals. This is all about "fixing it."

Movement of an Average Attribute to a Strength: This category is "common sense, but not often common practice." Why? Because we tend to equate development opportunities with "weaknesses" or things that need to be improved. In actuality, it is much easier and more motivating to begin coaching someone who has already demonstrated an acceptable behavior or skill, and look for opportunities to either use that behavior more frequently or in more depth. The Leader is already beginning from a solid foundation. This is all about "reinforcing it."

Overuse of a Strength: As individuals take on new roles which stretch them, they often continue to rely on the same skills and behaviors which they used in the past. They suddenly discover that what was once perceived as a "gift" to the organization is suddenly causing them to be ineffective. It is counter-intuitive to coach someone to stop displaying a strength; rather, as a Coach, you should strive to help them understand how to "turn down the dial a bit" to protect that strength. This typically occurs by either modulating the intensity or the frequency of that behavior. Other times, it may be developing a completely new behavior or skill, which had not been required until now, to "increase the number of tools in the toolkit." This is all about "dialing it down."

> "My Coach asks questions that make me stop and think about how I can approach things differently."

Leveraging a Strength Found in Others: Although individuals tend to default to personally addressing a development need within themselves, there are times where a Leader may choose to address a gap by consciously working with others who possess that attribute. In other words, choosing to "buy" vs. "make" that characteristic (which may mean hiring for this skill, finding a colleague or business partner with this skill, or partnering with someone else). We all have areas that we could address, but we do not have the desire to do it, and this is a potential solution. This is all about "buying it."

Demonstrating a Possessed but Unrecognized Attribute: This type of development action typically surfaces with a Leader who needs to gain more visibility or be more effective in promoting themselves within the organization, or with a Leader who is new to the team of the organization. In both cases, the Leader believes they possess a certain strength, but have not been able to display it in their current role. This is all about "exposing it."

To review, we have summarized five different types of professional development, and knowing how and what to coach for in each of these situations can be very effective.

It all begins with an observable behavior!

If this behavior …

> needs to be improved upon, then the Coaching will focus on "fixing it."

> needs to move from an average attribute to a strength, then the Coaching will focus on "reinforcing it."

> is overused, then the Coaching should focus on "dialing it down."

> is absent, and consequently this Leader needs to leverage a strength found in others, then the Coaching will focus on "buying" this skill elsewhere.

> is not recognized as a positive attribute that the Leader brings to the table, then the Coaching must focus on "exposing it" to become a visible strength.

Professional development tends to fall into one of these five categories. Regardless of the development need, the plan which the Leader develops must focus on having a measurable impact as a result of the behavior change.

"Your true character is revealed by the clarity of your convictions, the choices you make, and the promises you keep. Hold strongly to your principles and refuse to follow the currents of convenience. What you say and do defines who you are, and who you are ... forever."

Chapter 8
Am I Doing This "Right?" Practical Applications for Coaching Success

"What we can easily see is only a small percentage of what is possible. Imagination is having the vision to see what is just below the surface; to picture that which is essential, but invisible to the eye."

We are often asked, *"How do I know if I am doing this right?"* Great question!

It is often easier to answer that question by reminding you what coaching is not, and then ensuring that you are not falling into the traps that so frequently catch new Coaches. We have provided a list that highlights the most frequent mistakes that developing Coaches make. Reflect on this list periodically to make sure you are

> "GUIDE Coaching is a tool I can use to truly empower my team. I hadn't realized I was 'doing' too much and creating co-dependence by being such a 'go-to' person."

staying focused on the heart of coaching. As we have said before, you want to be the *"guide on the side, not the sage on the stage!"*

You are NOT coaching when you are ...

Jumping to "fixing" ... *to understand is critical and provides context.*

The number one mistake new Coaches make is turning a potential coaching moment into advice giving or telling. Most new Coaches need to "bite their tongue", be more curious by asking more questions, and self-manage their tendency/habit of wanting to give an answer. Sometimes the solution is so clear to us that we want to shout it out, but it's much more sustainable and likely to resonate with the Leader if they come up with it, not you.

Not really identifying the desired outcome/vision ... *think of the iceberg.*

New Coaches often make assumptions based on their paradigm or experience. When we make assumptions in our understanding, we miss identifying the underlying or explicitly desired outcome or vision. This needs to come from the Leader, not us, and we get there by asking questions up front about what the Leader wants – either in the long term or in the short term – and by being curious about why this is so important to the Leader.

Not linking to vision and values ... *the "hook" for alignment and engagement.*

We have talked a lot about the "hook," and it is vitally important to find "the hook" in every coaching encounter. People will not change their behavior or take any action forward until they see "what's in it for them." The "hook" is the "what's in it for them." Whether it is a small issue or a life-changing decision, Leaders need to link it somehow to their goals, their vision, and their values. As Coaches, your job is to discover that which is important to your Leader and refer to them often either as reassurance of a tough decision they are making, or to re-direct them if they are heading down a path that does not align with what is important to them. "Finding the hook" is especially important when you are coaching someone you perceive as being an unwilling Leader. It is even more important to get them to understand "what's in it for them," to "own" the feedback, and to be motivated to move forward.

Doing all the talking ... *ratio should be 80/20.*

If you find that you are talking more than you are listening, you are not coaching. Remember, you have two ears and one mouth for a reason! We have said this before, and we will say it again: *"Your role as a Coach is not to say something brilliant, but rather to ask thoughtful questions."* It is not to be the *"sage on the stage, but the guide on the side."* You know you are coaching when your Leader is talking more than you are (and you are listening more!).

Asking too many closed questions ... *ask thoughtful, open questions.*

The type of questions you ask really sets the tone for the coaching. Closed questions require simple, one- or two-word answers and leave little for your Leader to expand upon. Open questions are thoughtful, thought-provoking, and require your Leader to think and express more. Closed questions often indicate that the Coach has the end or solution in mind: *"Have you thought about ... ?"* is really a cleverly disguised statement similar to *"I think you should do this ..."*

Thinking too much ... *stay curious; keep the questions simple and open.*

We often find that new Coaches struggle with "being in their head too much" and attempting to think of the next brilliant question. Or a new Coach may be thinking about how they have dealt with a similar problem in the past, which means they are neither listening to the words the Leader is saying or picking up on their tone of voice or non-verbal clues. Stay curious, and go with the flow of the conversation. Avoid being overly structured or following the process to an extreme. Like coaching, the GUIDE Coaching process is only an overall roadmap: the priority is where the Leader wants to arrive.

Getting too much detail and history ... *coaching is "forwarding."*

When you find that you are getting irrelevant information and the conversation strays towards details of events versus impact on the Leader, then you know you are mired in too much detail. Ask yourself or your Leader how or why this is relevant. Remember, it turns into therapy when you and your Leader are focused too much on the past. And, since you do not have to write a novel based on the situation, all of the details really do not matter. Ask yourself whether you have enough context. If yes, then proceed. GUIDE Coaching is about forwarding the Leader to action, not reliving the past.

Taking monkeys on your back ... *it is their situation to take on and own all of the issues.*

On the one hand, taking on the actions and issues for your Leader will be hard to resist for those of you who are connection-oriented and truly desire to help your Leader. On the other hand, those of you who "want to move things along" and drive action tend to take ownership for your Leaders' actions as well. Always remember that it is their situation to own, so the Leader needs to take the actions. You are not helping if you "take their monkeys" or "fix" the problems for them.

Not self-managing ... *know your biases – it's all about them, not you.*

A self-aware Coach is an unbiased Coach. If you know yourself, you know what to watch out for and where you need to stretch yourself to be more effective. Remember, coaching is not about you; it is about your Leader. Strive to adapt your style to fit what your Leader needs from you. Avoid automatically coaching others the way you would want to be coached. Instead, know your Leader well enough to assess what coaching style will work best for them.

We have touched on what most Coaches do when they are NOT coaching!

Here is what you will want to check for to be sure that you ARE being the best Coach you can be!

✓ Remember, the process is theoretically linear, yet ambiguous in practice. How long you spend in each step is situational, and you may go up and down the process throughout coaching.

✓ You may not cover each step in every coaching session. Some steps require more thought and "homework" (for the Leader!) between coaching sessions, and that is OK.

✓ You may need to educate your Leader (e.g., what coaching is and is not) to align expectations (e.g., *"I know you want advice, but as your Coach I want to first facilitate your ideas."*).

✓ Knowing your Leader's motivators, values, priorities, goals, aspirations, etc. is imperative. These are the magnets to their choices and foster the greatest impact.

✓ The GUIDE Coaching model errs on the side of questioning versus problem solving. You do not need to be the problem-solver, in spite of the fact that this is likely a well-developed personal characteristic, and the reason why you have been successful in your organization.

✓ There are no right or wrong questions, just as there are no right or wrong answers. Don't become fixated on asking the "next best question" of your Leader. Trust your gut. The goal is not to "be right" but to move the Leader forward toward their visions, goals and/or desired outcomes.

✓ Ask open-ended, simple questions versus closed and leading questions to prompt the Leader's thoughts and ideas, and to gain clarification. You will be amazed at what you get when you ask those open-ended questions for which you think you know the answer. When you receive something completely different from your Leader, you both have an "ah-ha moment."

✓ Resist the immediate urge to "tell." Shift your internal paradigm. Get rid of that voice that tells you that *"you should have the answer,"* and become comfortable with not always having the answer (or not always sharing "your answer").

✓ Watch your biases, know your style, and self-manage accordingly. Remember you have intrinsic strengths as a Coach, and also things that would be identified as cautions. Your style, perspective and choices may not work for them. Be mindful.

✓ Maintain a supportive approach but ask the "tough" questions to foster reflection and/or actions toward the Leader's vision and desired outcomes. Too often we are afraid to ask that tough question because we do not want to be abrasive. We think it might be too personal, or we are afraid of the answer. As a Coach, ask it! It is the tough questions that often lead to those break-through answers that can make the difference between treading water and moving forward with positive momentum.

✓ Do not make assumptions, but rather ask questions to validate. Just because you think you understand the issue or know what your Leader is thinking, you should ask additional questions to validate your hypotheses. You may be surprised at the assumptions you made, which in fact do not hold true.

✓ Paraphrase and summarize often to gain clarity and foster buy-in toward choices. By doing this, you ensure that you and your Leader do not go so far down the same track, but in different directions. It makes sense to touch base and make sure you are both moving in the same direction and are on-board with the objectives. Occasionally "check-in" with your Leader regarding what they need from you as a Coach.

✓ There is a time for giving feedback within coaching. When giving feedback, focus on the objectives and why you are giving the feedback. Be cognizant of tangents or diversions that take you off-track, and be cautious to not make all of your coaching a direct feedback conversation.

✓ Give advice and offer perspective sparingly. Use judgment and always consider context. Your natural inclination may be to offer advice, especially if you have been through a similar situation in the past or have had to solve a similar problem. The criteria should be what is in the best interest of your Leader. Remember, what worked for you might not be what works for them.

✓ Become a fan of quiet spaces in conversation. Pauses are OK and often mean you have prompted the Leader to think and evaluate. Give your Leader the time to think. Don't feel the need to fill in that gap with your own words.

✓ Always ensure your Leader leaves with an action. This may be something to think about, someone to talk to, or something to do. This allows your Leader to be clear on accountability and action, and allows you to have a starting point on which to begin the next conversation. These "assignments" allow for more flow between sessions and foster accountability.

Are you "doing" this right? You will know when you are! It will feel "right." You will see the direct impact of your guiding and questioning. You will see your Leader's eyes light up as they uncover a solution or a perspective that they missed. You will find your team needs less of your time making

> "Success isn't a result of spontaneous combustion. You must set yourself on fire."
> -Arnold H. Glasow

decisions for them as they become more engaged. You will find people flock to you as your reputation for building a strong team and being a great Leader grows within the organization.

"Those who are touched by an inspirational idea and allow it to take charge and dominate their thoughts find new vistas open to them. Inspired thinking releases power to carry you the distance and as long as enthusiasm lasts, so will new opportunities, adding significance to all you do."

Chapter 9
Measuring the ROI of Coaching

"The rock that is an obstacle in the path of one person becomes a stepping stone in the path of another."

How do you measure the effectiveness of coaching? What is the ROI of coaching? How do you know if it is "paying off?"

The idea of quantifying coaching is the proverbial "million-dollar" question.

Coaching is about change. Someone wants to change a behavior, a job, or a way they are approaching an issue. Shouldn't that be the first measurement for the success of coaching? Did the needed change occur? Yes or no?

Asking targeted questions of the Leader and/or his colleagues may help to determine the success of the coaching engagement. These questions can range from being very subjective to approaching a more objective and cost/value based approach.

1. Ask your Leader what she thought of being coached ...
   "where did it meet, exceed, or fall short of expectations?"

2. Ask your Leader what she learned during the process ...
   "what is new or different as a result of her 'ah-ha' moments?"

3. Ask your Leader and others she works with (a 360° view from managers, peers/colleagues, and direct reports) ...
   "what skills or new ideas was she able to immediately apply to her job/position? What changes or improvements were noticeable to others?"

4. Ask the Leader's Leaders ...
   "define what changes in productivity or tangible results have been observed since the coaching began."

Let's say you are coaching a manager to be a better Leader on his team – challenging him to provide really specific and concise training, development and feedback so that they are more effective in their roles. "How do you measure your effectiveness?" At the most basic level, you would identify the benefit of the coaching. This may be looking at metrics, such as increased sales, number of employees rated as "top talent" who were promoted or retained, or how much they improved their score on the company employee attitude survey. You get the picture!

> "Obstacles are those frightful things you see when you take your eyes off your goals."

The International Coach Federation (ICF), founded in 1995, is the leading global organization dedicated to advancing the coaching profession. The ICF Global Coaching Client Study of 2009 found that coaching does indeed increase organizational ROI percentage in the range of 700%! ICF also found that executives who were coached for a minimum of six months experienced a 77% improvement in their working relationships with direct reports, 71% with supervisors, and 63% with peers. They found job satisfaction rose by 61%, and organizational commitment increased by 44%.

While the above numbers reference formal external coaching engagements, consider the benefits you as an internal Coach can provide:

• Increases in productivity and team effectiveness.

- Increases in overall job satisfaction by creating an empowering and more autonomous work environment where team members want to work hard.

- Increases in customer satisfaction scores as team members are more aligned and engaged.

- Decreases in turnover because people are happier at work with clear feedback, focused development, intentional support, and more thoughtful relationships.

These are incredible numbers. Some people love statistics. Others are skeptical. We all know that statistics can be presented to make any kind of case! Regardless, we can reasonably extrapolate that coaching does provide a benefit to the organization. Sometimes, this can be measured in terms of a true ROI percentage and other times, it manifests itself in more subjective results.

"This is the beginning of a new day. You have been given this day to use as you will. You can waste it or use it for good. What you do today is important because you are exchanging a day of your life for it. When tomorrow comes, this day will be gone forever; in its place is something that you have left behind ... let it be something good."

Chapter 10
Coaching Today: Virtually and Globally

"Different people. Different beliefs. Different hopes. Different dreams ... we have become not just a melting pot, but a beautiful mosaic."

It is difficult enough to be an effective Coach when you are engaging with someone in person, but the reality is that you are likely leading virtual teams or working in a global matrix where you may have to influence others you have never physically met. While making an effort to physically "stand in your Leader's shoes" to "meet them where they are" is a valuable return on your investment (particularly in the *Grounding* or *Understanding* phases), you certainly will not be able to be face-to-face in every instance.

Where you can, leverage technology. Communication research has shown that 50% of what we communicate (intentionally or unintentionally) is manifested in our body language. Skype, WebEx, or any other type of "video chat" enables you to read body language to help you to better sense where your Leader is emotionally at any given time and to sense that which is "unsaid."

You can coach effectively over the phone, but it is certainly more difficult! First, you absolutely cannot multi-task while coaching, so if you are compelled to look at every email the minute it "chimes" on your laptop, make sure you turn it off before coaching. Better yet, consider leaving your office to place yourself in an environment that allows you to clear your mind and focus solely on your Leader.

One of the biggest challenges to coaching over the phone is to be conscious of and comfortable with silence. Often times your Leader is thinking or processing. You need to give them time to do that versus "jumping in" and begin talking simply to "fill the quiet space." Remember, the Leader should be doing the majority of the work, and the majority of the talking! If you are unsure how to interpret the silence, do not be afraid to ask what the other person is doing versus assuming they are stuck and proceeding to fill the void in the conversation.

Since visual cues are absent on the phone, your auditory senses need to kick into high gear. Research shows that another 40% of what we communicate is transmitted through the tone of our voice. Pay particular attention to changes in how the Leader sounds, whether it is during the call or compared to prior calls. Remember, coaching is about using your intuition, so if the person sounds different from how they typically are, do not hesitate to vocalize your observation. Your hunch may be right, or it may be nothing. Either way, it may open a door to some deeper findings.

As a Coach, you should also be conscious of your own signals that are sent across the phone. If you feel yourself "fading," that is losing interest or focus, get out of your chair and move around. Walking or gesturing while talking really does transmit energy over the phone lines! Be extra cognizant of the speed of your communication or your use of idioms or slang if you are coaching someone whose native language is different from yours. Again, it is all about the Leader, so make sure to consciously check-in to ensure understanding versus assuming you understand or have been understood. One of the best ways to do this is to check for clarification if something is unclear to you, or ask the

> "Senses, intuition and active listening skills need to be on high alert!"

Leader to highlight key take-aways in their own words to ensure you have communicated effectively.

Virtual Coaching Tips

- Use technology whenever possible: WebEx, Skype, Video Chat, etc.

- Invest in "face-to-face" time for Grounding.

- Establish ground rules such as no multi-tasking, emailing, etc.

- Embrace pauses, count to 10, and ASK what's going on … silence means many things, so don't assume!

- Listen for and pay attention to change in tone of voice.

- Inquire, check-in and ask for "feedback" frequently. Watch biases and maintain 80/20 ratio (i.e., you talking 20% of the time).

- Maintain your body language – stand up … it keeps you engaged! Be cognizant of facial expressions … they come across regardless of the medium!

Coaching people from different cultures also adds a level of complexity. While we certainly do not want you to generalize and thus inadvertently stereotype different cultures, you do need to be conscious of cultural differences. From our experience coaching Leaders around the world, there are differences in personal comfort levels when recognizing individual accomplishments, "pushing back" hierarchically, giving developmental feedback to others, and discussing their lives outside of work. Interestingly enough, we tend to see cultural differences more at lower levels of an organization. Once people get to mid-level

> "I'm from Beijing, and can say that GUIDE Coaching transcends international boundaries. It has helped me to adjust and clarify my goals and ensures that positive behavior change is sustainable."

leadership roles, they gravitate towards displaying the behaviors which their company values more than those from their home country.

This does not mean you should use cultural differences as an excuse to not ask important questions. It just means that it may take more time to "get below the tip of the iceberg" during the *Grounding* or *Understanding* phases of GUIDE Coaching.

Culture, Background, Style and Situation are all Context

- We tend to coach others the way we prefer to be coached, as opposed to how they would like to be coached.

- Pay attention to introversion or extroversion. It impacts comfort levels in inquiry.

- Become skilled at adapting your methods, techniques, and approaches ... both personally and contextually.

- Use open and closed questions wisely ... closed questions tend to lead.

- Learn the fundamentals of listening, empathizing, probing, and contextualizing. We tend to revert to advice-giving, problem-solving, and theorizing.

- Common differences between cultures include:

  - Comfort articulating individual accomplishments or perceived "negative" information.

  - Comfort discussing personal background and sharing personal information in *Grounding*.

  - Communication style, body language, eye contact, and energy.

- Be sensitive to language fluency. Slow down, avoid slang and do not assume understanding.

"We are committed to be the best, with the full power of all that we are, we will go where there is no path and blaze a trail. Our positive attitude will be a powerful force that cannot be stopped."

Chapter 11
More About Assessment, Development, and Coaching

"A true leader has the confidence to stand alone, the courage to make tough decisions, and the compassion to listen to the needs of others. He does not set out to be a leader, but becomes one by the quality of his actions and the integrity of his intent."

When asked to define what we do at ISHR Group, we reply in terms of defining our three "buckets"— namely, our expertise in leadership assessment, leadership development, and leadership coaching.

Leadership Assessment

When we started ISHR Group in 1999, our primary service was "leadership assessment," and this remains a key focus in our business today. Our practice area in leadership assessment helps organizations identify critical success factors which differentiate, and serve to develop, high performers and top talent. Featuring comprehensive personal assessment interviews, Live 360°s, and comprehensive feedback assessing strengths and development needs, our leadership assessment process is a powerful predictor of leadership performance and an invaluable enabler for personal and professional growth. Our business was founded on providing third-party assessment services for our clients as we helped them to identify and develop their high-potential candidates. We also built a tremendous business in the area of teaching Human Resource (HR) Leaders across the globe this four-step assessment process, which enables them to complete in-house assessments directly.

Our clients leverage our leadership assessment expertise when they need a more robust process for identifying and developing the high-potential talent within their organizations, when they need help developing certain individuals who they believe could take on a larger role, or if they are looking to develop a comprehensive talent management program to begin to identify their bench strength. As senior HR Leaders, they recognize that strong assessment skills are perhaps the most important competency that their Human Resource Managers could possess. They ask us to help "raise the bar" on the assessment skills of their HRMs, to help them assess talent within their organizations, help to promote the right people, and help to make the right hiring decisions.

Our customized practice area in leadership assessment helps organizations:

- Identify critical success factors that differentiate high performers.
- Translate existing company values into observable behaviors that can be assessed against.
- Develop organization review processes to assess the talent pipeline at various levels.
- Calibrate talent standards globally.
- Train internal HRMs to conduct leadership assessments and deliver effective feedback and coaching.
- Provide third-party leadership assessments and ongoing coaching for key Leaders at all levels in the organization.

Our consulting expertise tells us that our leadership assessment process is comprised of the following steps:

1. *Historical Interview:* An intense conversation covering personal background, education, professional experience, and career goals to gain insight into how a person became the Leader they are today and where they aspire to go in the future.

2. *Live 360°:* Confidential conversations with managers, peers, business partners, and subordinates with whom the Leader works to provide additional insight and perspective as to the individual's strengths and development needs.

3. *Leadership Assessment and Development Report:* Comprehensive written reports summarize and interpret the data gained through the interview and Live 360°, including background information, a detailed presentation of strengths and development needs, and career advice to serve as a foundation for on-going coaching.

4. *Coaching:* Intense personal coaching and feedback sessions (ranging from 3-12 months) address the themes surfaced during the assessment process, whether it is leveraging a strength, enhancing a skill, or addressing a development opportunity. Feedback is professionally and respectfully delivered with a focus on actionable development plans, which may result in a follow-up 360°, leader assimilation, or team-building session as appropriate.

Leadership assessment is how we got started and is still a large part of our business today. We are thrilled to say it evolved with us. We know assessment works because of countless comments like this, *"This was undoubtedly a life altering experience ... my 'ah-ha moment' ... I finally understand the feedback, and what to do about it ... everyone should be given this opportunity."*

Leadership Development

We had been active in the world of leadership assessment for several years when one of our clients asked us to design and deliver a week-long leadership development program. We were up for that challenge. After years of completing assessments on all different levels, across all different functions and industries, across all different parts of the globe, we had gained tremendous insight into the world of leadership: what made for great Leaders, and not-so-great Leaders. As a result of the insight we gained, we created a model that we call *"Triple A Leadership"* that you will learn more about in Chapter 12.

"Triple A Leadership" became our leadership foundation for what we had learned as a result of completing thousands of comprehensive leadership assessments around the world and at all different levels, functions, and industries. We took *"Triple A Leadership"* and used it as a baseline framework for creating our leadership development curriculum. This data was rich. It was steeped in reality, and steeped in the real stories we heard as we completed leadership assessments around the world. We used this "inside-knowledge" to create a fast-track, industry-acclaimed series of "experiences" that run the gamut on developing and refining leadership skills in an invigorating and interactive manner. Building on the concept that superior Leaders possess superior self-awareness, we work with each client to create a customized program and design "learning laboratories" where Leaders can explore their styles, increase self-awareness, and develop business-critical skills.

Based on our discoveries and our development of *"Triple A Leadership,"* our clients tasked us with developing a holistic leadership development curriculum based on specific needs of Leaders at each leadership level. They wanted our programs to be comprehensive, contemporary, interactive, and customized. Today, our team of ISHR consultants creates and delivers learning experiences that transcend the classroom and "make it real" by creating Leaders who not only grow via the experience, but in turn instill growth in those around them to have a ripple effect in their organizations.

Our clients began to call our leadership development programs "edgy." To us, to be called "edgy" was a compliment. It was validation that we were delivering an uncommon experience. Our edge was that we provided an interactive and supportive forum for participants to transcend their comfort zones and stretch themselves to reach higher learning levels. We don't design "off the shelf" courses — never have, and never will. Our courses are experiences, rich with immediately applicable content and concepts. While each course is customized to address client-specific needs, the common denominators are our foundational beliefs and our adaptability.

Today, we act as the "Leadership University" for several of our clients. We design and deliver multiple-level leadership development programs, starting with new Leaders and focusing on personal leadership, then moving to influential leadership, advanced leadership, and senior leadership experiences. We provide customized content to every client with whom we work. We not only design and deliver content for these programs, but we also project manage the programs, ranging in length from two days to two weeks.

Participants in our programs have told us that they have attended numerous leadership training courses and found them to be either too theoretical or too fuzzy to have much application or impact when they returned to their offices. They reported that ours was unique. We commit to making all of our talent development experiences hands-on, real-life, and practical. All of our leadership courses are facilitated by our team of Coaches who foster challenging introspection and practical application before, during, and after the experience. Where else could our clients find a leadership development program that consistently delivered customized and applicable skill development that was able to be put to use immediately by each course participant?

Our goal is to make these leadership experiences "sticky." We have all been to programs where we leave on a Friday afternoon feeling energized and ready to make some changes. We are ready to try new things and take on the world. Yet by Tuesday, we are back in the office, fighting fires, dealing with issues, and all of the ambition and enthusiasm that we had when we left the program, all of the commitments and goals that we made, have all but disappeared.

Several years ago, we decided to try something new, and it has become the hallmark of our leadership development experiences. We know coaching works. We know accountability works. We know time allows for traction. We began to include pre- and post-course coaching into all of our programs. We now meet with and talk to our course participants before the program even begins to help build that comfort level and those relationships so that when the program begins, people are ready to engage immediately. We reduced the valuable time it takes for people to get familiar with the feel of a group before they decide to engage.

As we would observe and work with each participant during the course of the program, we found we were able to provide valuable insight that was readily accepted because we had taken the time to build the relationships and trust up front.

Most importantly, we continue to work with each course participant after the program has ended. Doesn't this make all the sense in the world? We know what their goals and commitments are as they leave the program. We know their strengths and development needs, how they interacted, and what they took away from the program. We continue to work with them post-course to make sure what they learned has some "stickiness" – that staying power – that makes the difference between something that was nice to learn, but soon forgotten, and something that becomes an integral part of someone's leadership DNA and how they operate.

Leadership Coaching

As our leadership assessment process evolved, we suggested to our clients that they would get a greater return on their investment if we continued to work with each Leader beyond the one "feedback" session. Our rationale was that we now knew that person better than anyone else in the organization – their strengths, their development needs, their aspirations, and their concerns. Continuing to work with our assessees made all the sense in the world!

As leadership Coaches, we knew that in order for behavior change to occur, there needed to be a built-in accountability process to ensure that new discoveries were indeed implemented. Leadership coaching provides that extra level of personal development so often needed to provide vision and clarity to personal development and goals, regardless of whether it is done in conjunction with an assessment, with a development program, or as a stand-alone initiative.

> "Receiving this assessment, and being coached by you, has been 'a gift' … thank you for helping me to grow and develop in my career. This has been life-changing."

We began coaching Leaders in a variety of situations. We were asked to coach high-potential, emerging Leaders to make them even more likely to assume key leadership roles in the future. We would work with a key individual who was struggling with building a high-performing team. We provided coaching to that individual and to the team in terms of how to work together more effectively as they dealt with issues pertaining to communicating, decision making, handling conflict, or influencing behaviors. Often times, we would work with acquisition and integration teams to coach Leaders through the dance of merging two newly combined corporate cultures. Frequently, we would work with new Leaders to help them hit the ground running as quickly as possible in their new role so that they make the biggest impact and minimize their learning curve.

Our clients told us what differentiated us from other Coaches was:

• Our combination of strong coaching skills and consulting expertise based on our corporate HR careers, global coaching experience focusing on leadership effectiveness, and our encouraging, but direct, style.

• Our over-arching methodology, which is built into our unique coaching process. We utilize data gleaned from an in-depth "get to know you" session, verbal 360°, and a psychological profile. Our coaching process allows flexibility in each phase tailored to each individual's needs and objectives.

• Our focus on observable behavior change enhancing an individual's leadership effectiveness. We have a passion for helping Leaders be as effective as they can be, whether they are successful Leaders wanting to become even more effective in larger roles, or whether they are Leaders struggling in their current role.

• Pre- and post-coaching benchmarks to assess the impact of the coaching engagement.

And, of course, our experience with all of this – the assessments, our development programs, and our years of coaching, led to our insight that all Leaders can and should become Coaches within their organizations. We know that is the best way to build that sought-after goal of increased alignment and engagement that every organization, and every Leader, seeks from every employee! What you have just read is our discovery of the value of creating a true culture of coaching. The result of that insight was the creation of our GUIDE Coaching model and process! Clearly, you know what happened next!

"Sometimes great knowledge lies in the discovery of something we did not anticipate, something that enlightens us to a new perspective. Then we are changed and enriched. Real discovery is a stairway that requires our participation, and begs us to climb, and climb some more."

Chapter 12
What Makes a Great Leader? "Triple A Leadership"

"Watch your thoughts, for they become words. Choose your words, for they become actions. Understand your actions, for they become habits. Study your habits, for they will become your character. Develop your character, for it becomes your destiny"

In the last chapter, we referenced how our work completing leadership assessments led to creating our *"Triple A Leadership"* model! This chapter is devoted to explaining the characteristics of a *"Triple A Leader:"* namely, those characteristics which differentiate superior Leaders around the world.

As our business evolved and we worked with more and more Leaders around the world, spanning all functions and industries, all ages and genders, all educational levels, it became very apparent to us that leadership was "all about that individual." In fact, we have a sign hanging in our office that says, "It's all about me."

Some people may view this as a bratty sign befitting a selfish teenager. We see it as an expression of truth. For some of you, the concept of leadership truly being "all about you" may fly in the face of what you have read about successful Leaders — that they need to have specific attributes and styles to be successful, or that they create such high-performing teams that they become unnecessary. At the end of the day, leadership, and your leadership style, how it is presented, its strengths, its weaknesses, its impact … is truly all about you! And, the more you know about "you," the more adept you can be in adapting your leadership style to be most effective for the situation and the individuals with whom you are interacting.

Although there are certainly common attributes of successful Leaders, we have found that they can come in all shapes, sizes, and styles. How you lead truly depends on who you are, so the first step is to genuinely understand yourself. *"Have you taken the time over the past few years to reflect back on what you have done, and why you have done it? What have you learned over the years about what you like and don't like about your roles? What have you accomplished — more importantly, what attributes have caused you to be successful or to struggle? What are the common themes of feedback you have received over the years?"* These are factors and questions we typically prompt Leaders to reflect upon during an extensive assessment interview to identify patterns of behavior and preferences over time.

> "I don't know the key to success, but the key to failure is trying to please everybody."
> -Bill Cosby

Now that you know yourself, to what extent does that match the perception others have of you? *"Are you in the habit of asking for feedback from a 360° view? Are you getting feedback from your managers, peers, and people who work for you? Are you making sure it is specific and balanced? Are you getting both positive and developmental or constructive feedback on how you can be most effective?"*

Although asking for feedback and knowing how you are perceived sounds like common sense, it is not common practice. It may be uncomfortable at first, but if you get in the habit of sincerely asking for feedback and then sincerely doing something about it — leveraging your strengths and responding to suggestions to improve your effectiveness — people will see you as sincerely caring about their input and be more open to suggestions the next time.

Not surprisingly, the most common coaching point is "managing perception." Like it or not, perception is reality in any organization, and you can not determine to what extent you should focus on changing a perception unless you know "the book on you" — what it is and how you want it to read.

Having assessed and coached hundreds of Leaders across the globe, we are often asked, *"What are the common characteristics of successful Leaders?"* After analyzing the data we have collected over the past decade through our assessment and coaching practice, we have summarized what we have come to call *"Triple A Leadership."* In this model, the A's stand for: "Accountable," "Attitude" and "Approach." It is important to note that *"Triple A Leadership"* is not related to the stereotypical "Type A Personality," as we have found that any personality type or style can successfully display or demonstrate the A's associated with *"Triple A Leadership."*

The most common denominator and first level of *"Triple A Leaders"* is that they are "Accountable." They get things done, and they deliver in a credible manner. The next level is "Attitude." They have a positive and proactive attitude toward their work, their development, and the way they lead others. The third level is "Approach." This is where we find many Leaders continue to struggle to develop. "Approach" is all about how Leaders work with others and within the organization to achieve results.

Our observations of what *"Triple A Leadership"* is all about, are on the following pages. We hope you find them helpful, and perhaps you may use them as a roadmap for your own development. *"Triple A Leadership"* is not a "cookie cutter" approach. It is one that you can achieve by consciously stretching your style outside of your comfort zone to be most effective, while still being true to yourself by leveraging your strengths and preferences. Surprisingly, the majority of the Leaders we have assessed have never stopped to consider their preferences, where they wanted to go from a career perspective, and the gaps they needed to fill to reach their goals. Most have had a sponsor who has called them and told them what job to go to next. While having sponsors is certainly important, it can lead to issues when the sponsor leaves the company or perhaps falls out of favor within the organization. Many Leaders realize too late that they are not satisfied in their careers, have not built a broad network, or have pigeon-holed themselves unintentionally, by having a passive approach to their own development.

Single A: "Accountable"

This is what we refer to as the "ticket to entry" in any discussion of leadership and provides the potential to assume larger roles in an organization. These are the basic elements of "getting it done" and delivering results for the organization. In addition, these are the elements that bring attention to many new Leaders early in their careers. Being "Accountable" doesn't "go away" or become less important as a Leader moves up in *"Triple A Leadership,"* but rather becomes the foundation and the common denominator for all successful Leaders. Simply put, they are driven, motivated, and focused on delivering above and beyond expectations.

- *High "Say-Do" Ratio:* This is doing what you say you are going to do. It is being dependable, delivering results, and meeting or exceeding performance objectives.

- *Credible:* This is being believable. It is being seen as doing the right thing versus having any hidden agenda. It means that you have built a solid foundation of experience and that you are speaking from a base of knowledge.

- *Critical Thinker:* This means being able to analyze data, options, and input to make decisions. It's about asking questions to understand and being thoughtful about gathering data. It also means knowing when to stop gathering input and proceeding to "make the call."

- *Adaptable:* This is having the flexibility to adapt to internal changes within the organization or external fluctuations in the marketplace. It means you see change as a positive, as an opportunity to unearth new possibilities, as opposed to being resistant to consider new approaches.

- *Resourceful:* This is not necessarily having the highest IQ, but rather having the resourcefulness and know-how to figure out how to get up to speed quickly in any new situation. This can be through self-study or through leveraging the knowledge of others. This is also about "getting it done," even without the optimal number of resources, money or time.

Double A: "Attitude"

"Double A Leaders" are not only "Accountable," but they also have an outstanding "Attitude" and a quiet confidence (humility) towards themselves, others, and their work that gets them noticed. These are attributes that differentiate them from their peers. Simply put, these Leaders are passionate, always learning, decisive in their views, and possess a healthy maturity.

- *Managerial Courage:* This is about making decisions, even the tough calls. It's about having the courage of your conviction to present or support an unpopular view. It's about considering multiple variables, and knowing when to continue discussion, and when to take action.

- *Maturity:* This has nothing to do with age or experience, but with "being comfortable in your own skin." It's about having the self-awareness to know the key strengths that cause you to be effective and those developmental areas which you need to address to be even more effective. This is about owning your mistakes versus finger-pointing or placing blame.

- *Continuous Learner:* This implies possessing a positive and proactive attitude toward your own personal growth and development. It means being curious, not complacent. It is about seeing personal and organizational development as a journey versus a destination. It is seeking out and being open to feedback and ideas from others and the willingness to stretch yourself versus staying in your comfort zone.

- *Passionate:* This is genuinely loving the work you are doing and having an infectious enthusiasm that entices others to want to work with and for you. It's about having the ability to build a following and having people say, "I don't care what the job is; I just want to work for that person again." It's about radiating a positive, "can-do," "glass half-full" attitude. When someone doesn't love what they do, it shows in how they go about their day, and not surprisingly, it affects their ability to deliver. Leaders who genuinely love what they do seem to do their work with ease, and it impacts those around them more positively. When you do what you love, you are more productive and fulfilled.

Triple A: "Approach"

As you would expect, there are areas where even the most successful Leaders continually struggle and aspire to reach. Operating at the *"Triple A"* level is all about the "Approach" used to influence others and the organization.

We like to use the analogy of a conductor at this level of leadership. The conductor in an orchestra must divide his focus between the music, the instruments, and the musicians. While it is not necessary to know how to play all the instruments, the conductor must have an "ear" for the intended piece that he is conducting.

In leadership, this is analogous to having a vision that contains short-term elements, but also a long-term view. This is where we see most Leaders struggle. They have trouble letting go of the comfort of playing the instrument and learning to conduct (or influence) others to play toward the big picture strategy. Most Leaders are good at and have been rewarded for "playing in the orchestra." Stepping out of this can be a hard habit to break. It requires deliberate effort be more "Coach-like" in order to influence (rather than do) and guide others toward alignment and engagement. It requires a broader perspective, rather than a narrow or siloed view of their people and organization.

- *Big Picture Thinker:* Although well-intended, many Leaders get bogged down with daily firefighting or the transactional nature of their businesses and do not consciously carve out time to think long-term or set a vision for where they want their organization to go. This is all about focusing on the big picture, creating, and communicating a strategy. It's about being strategic, and taking a non-siloed approach. It means being able to wear the big hat regarding vision, goals, business "levers," processes, resources and talent. It means staying abreast of your environment as it relates to customers, industry, competition and the world. It means being able to come up with creative and innovative approaches and ideas.

- *Leadership Flexibility:* Staying true to who you are does not mean only having one style of leadership. It is easy to lead a team of people like you, but much more difficult, and infinitely more effective, to lead a diverse team of individuals. The idea is not to require them to change to your style, but for you to understand how best to influence and motivate them as individuals and as a total team. Effective Leaders possess the ability to adapt their leadership style to motivate various people, styles, and situations. It means being able to lead different functions and businesses versus just the one you "grew up in." It means being able to master the transition from "Über Individual Contributor" to being able to deliver through others by coaching and motivating—not doing.

- *Ability to Influence:* This goes well beyond interpersonal skills and encompasses organizational knowledge. This is knowing who the key stakeholders are and being able to flex your communication style to see things from their perspective to get buy-in. It's about having communication savviness. Most Leaders communicate well in specific scenarios, but many still focus on trying to be equally effective on all fronts. This is about learning to communicate with individuals, small groups, or large groups across all levels of an organization and in formal presentations or informal networking events. It's about having presence. Like it or not, the way in which you present yourself goes a long way towards forming people's impression of you as a Leader. This can be how you dress, how you speak, or the impression you leave. Many Leaders we coach want to prove they can be successful without this, but they end up being overlooked or misperceived because they are not "memorable."

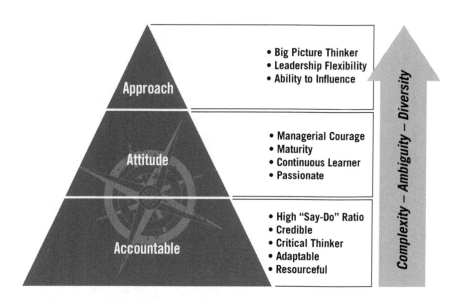

It is important to stress that as your span of influence increases and you reach higher levels within the organization, the levels of leadership don't go away. Rather, the "Complexity," "Ambiguity," and "Diversity" of decisions become even greater and broader. Leaders must adapt as expectations increase. The skills and characteristics for which Leaders achieved success early in their careers change over time. This evolution is not always natural, however, and requires self-awareness and a deliberate shift in behavior.

"Triple A Leadership" provides a snapshot of the common themes that emerged as we assessed Leaders across the globe. We have run this model past hundreds and thousands of people since we developed it, and we resoundingly hear, *"Yes! This makes sense."* People can review it, and quickly self-assess where they are in their own leadership development.

Are you a *"Triple A Leader?"* Are you "Accountable?" What is your "Attitude" toward your own development, development of others, and development of your work? What is your "Approach" towards others and to the organization?"

As you answer these questions for yourself and for those on your team and begin to move forward exploring how you can be a more effective Coach, we trust you will refer to *"Triple A Leadership,"* and use it as you apply the GUIDE Coaching model.

- We designed it to be a practical process!

- We designed it to be easily implemented by you and within your organization!

- We designed it to be a highly effective way to build alignment and engagement!

It is our hope and our goal that you embrace the fundamentals of GUIDE Coaching and move forward in building a highly aligned and engaged team. Thanks for reading!

"Our lives are not determined by what happens to us, but how we react to what happens; not by what life brings to us, but by the attitude we bring to life. A positive attitude causes a chain reaction of positive thoughts, events and outcomes. It is a catalyst ... a spark that creates extraordinary results."

For more Information …

We would love to hear from you about your success in using the GUIDE Coaching Model. If you would like to learn more about GUIDE Coaching or ISHR Group, please visit our website at www.ISHRGroup.com or contact us at info@ISHRGroup.com.

"The future doesn't just happen, it is created … our destiny is not in the stars, but in ourselves. We may need to follow in the wake of those who have gone before, but what we do and where we go is ultimately up to us. The attitude of initiative in an on-going state of exploration that is never finished … a journey that never ends."

Made in the USA
Middletown, DE
21 October 2015